FATHER TAKES A DRINK
&
Other Memories of Iran

HEYDAR RADJAVI

Mage Publishers

LIBRARY OF CONGRESS CATALOGING-IN-PUBLICATION DATA

978-1-949445-09-1

MAGE PUBLISHERS
AS@MAGE.COM
VISIT MAGE ONLINE AT WWW.MAGE.COM

Contents

*To my wife Ursula
for her constant encouragement*

*She has made an uncountable number
of comments and suggestions after each
reading of every story. They were very
valuable in clarifying certain passages
on complex cultural events, customs,
rituals, and ceremonies, especially those
unfamiliar to Western readers.*

*And to Marjan, Philip, Shirin, and
Carrie—representatives to us of the
younger generation to whose collective
lips this book hopes, as mentioned in the
preface, to bring understanding smiles.*

PREFACE

Most of the people who appear in these stories were known to me personally. We were all caught in the seemingly never-ending clashes between tradition and modernity that have defined Iran for more than a century. My elders and their contemporaries went through several great sociopolitical upheavals in the twentieth century, two of which were full-scale revolutions in 1906 and in 1979, both followed by devastating wars. My generation missed the first revolution and World War I, but witnessed many changes, including World War II, the experiments with democracy, and the attempts to nationalize the oil industry in the 1950s, culminating in the second revolution. The next generation experienced the most fundamental, and ultimately the most divisive, transitions in the recent history of the region. More than three of these generations populate the pages that follow.

I have tried to stick to my habitual light-hearted approach in putting together these sketches of personal history. I have failed in a few instances, though. Some important events just refused to be recalled with a light heart; sometimes anger desperately looked for an outlet, and I couldn't always ignore it.

Just as in my previous collection, *French Hats in Iran,* I have combined some minor characters to prevent congestion. Major characters I have treated with more respect. Many of them are easily identifiable. There are a few, including some in my own extended circle of family and friends, who could not be remembered kindly. Unless they were too well known as public figures, and thus impossible to protect, I have altered their names and addresses to save potential embarrassment to them and their offspring. One exception to this rule is Lady Saria the Pious, my best childhood friend's grandmother, whose parental strictures made early life nearly unbearable for my friend and his teenage mother, and whose unsolicited religious guidance offended almost everybody in our close-knit community. Yet I dare not camouflage her. When you get to know her in this book, if you haven't already done so in my earlier stories, I think you will agree with me: Lady Saria, who never told a lie, never used makeup, and never suffered fools gladly, would insist on appearing here either totally unadorned or not at all. I can't afford the latter choice. She is too essential to my narrative. And I still remember her with that strange mixture of respect and fear she instilled in me as a child.

Great tragedies endured by the people of Iran in the several decades past have resulted in highly bitter debates about causes and effects. The differences of opinion have now grown to apparently eternal enmities among various, mutually opposing, sections of the population. If you find yourself loyally and unconditionally clinging to any pole of opinion, you should be warned. Not every report in this book will amuse you; experience with my earlier stories tells me so. But I can promise you one thing, if it is any consolation. When you find a paragraph objectionable, keep reading, and you'll soon encounter another; it'll be equally objectionable, but this time to a dedicated opponent of yours. Whether or not you stop reading the book, please don't hide it from your children. How can it hurt them to have a nonpartisan glimpse into the undeniable cultural mayhem depicted here? Besides, I bet they can smile, more easily than we ourselves can, at what they will definitely come to view as the older generations' incredible eccentricities. May their generation smile together.

Father Takes a Drink

"Father is going to get drunk now, isn't he?" I asked Mother, no longer able to hide my anxiety. Father had just imbibed his first alcoholic beverage in his long life. He looked very nervous. Mother was biting her lip. I knew right away, from my parents' embarrassed and silent reaction, that my question shouldn't have been posed at all. Father was seventy-five years old, and Mother just under forty. I was almost nine. Father, having complained of persistent fatigue for months, had finally decided, with extreme reluctance, to obey his doctor's orders. The daring doctor had prescribed a small dose of cognac, this impure and evil substance, to be stirred into tea and taken after every evening meal for several weeks.

It was a cold winter evening. The three of us were sitting around our traditional *kursi* to keep warm. This highly efficient heating device, used in the family room of nearly every home in my hometown of Tabriz since time immemorial, was still a constant feature of winter living in the 1940s, the only exceptions being a few ultramodern households. The kursi came in various sizes—ours was a large one, an eight-seater—but its shape was invariable. It consisted of a low, square, four-legged wooden table with a large comforter covering it and extending amply on all sides. Divans and cushions provided cozy seating arrangements around the kursi, where you could snuggle under the comforter and read, write, chat, eat, or take a nap. The source of heat was a brazier, placed centrally under the device. It was filled with ashes that surrounded red-hot pieces of charcoal in the middle, and kept them, as Mother would put it, "on call." Periodically, as the need arose, Mother would carefully rearrange the ashes to expose a few "live" red pieces to produce more heat. The brazier was also used to keep food and snacks warm. (My favorite snack was potatoes buried in the brazier's hot ashes and slowly dry-baked to crisp perfection.) Only our close friends and relatives were entertained around the kursi. Our more formal guest room, one of Father's few concessions to modernity, had a wood-burning fireplace instead. It also had chairs and tables instead of floor cushions.

We had just finished supper, and Mother had gathered the dirty dishes off the top of the kursi, when Father drank his first cup of cognac-fortified tea which led to my anxious and impertinent question. The fortification consisted of pouring one tablespoonful of cognac into a cup of tea. After taking this polluted medicine, and before placing the little bottle of cognac safely on the highest and least accessible shelf on the far wall of the large living room, Father put the bottle of cognac in a bowl—so no single drop of the forbidden fluid could escape the container and, God forbid, contaminate the shelf or the wall, which would be very difficult to cleanse properly. He then took the spoon and the teacup to the courtyard and enlisted my help in washing them correctly in our flower garden. To observe the necessary purification ritual, he held the polluted objects in his hands, away from his person, close to the dirt on the ground—to prevent unwanted spattering. When signaled by him, I poured clean water upon them, three times, from an *aftafa*, the special watering can that is a must in every pious household. Then he took the aftafa into his own hand and cleansed his mouth and lips in the same manner. To protect our limbs from the freezing evening temperatures, the aftafa, filled with water, had fortunately been kept warm under the kursi—safely tied to one of the kursi's legs, so my cat, usually lounging in the cozy enclosure, couldn't easily topple it. The ritual cleansing done, we rushed back to our kursi to warm ourselves up.

I couldn't stop thinking about my innocent but improper question at the kursi and what had occasioned it. I was still silently praying for Father not to get drunk, or if he did, not to cause the kind of trouble drunkards reportedly did. Wasn't I always instructed not to go to the modern parts of the city, where the liquor stores and bars were located, especially after dark, even accompanied by grownups? Hadn't Mash Karim, the leatherworker, normally a very well-behaved man, gotten drunk only a few weeks earlier and beaten up his kids for no good reason at all? I wasn't even sure about my mother's own cousin Tahra's husband. He was a traveling salesman who, according to confidential reports from Tahra to Mother, not to be repeated to Father under any circumstances, drank regularly. And always came home from his sojourns, usually spent in the capital city, with a suitcase full of bottles of the evil medicine. He never bought it from the local stores in Tabriz—to prevent possible misunderstandings by his business associates. Father's new prescription made me think about Tahra's husband again:

he must have been misbehaving at home. Otherwise, why was Tahra spending so much time at our place recently, and staying overnight sometimes, even while her husband was in town? My older brother Bagher had tried to assure me that nothing untoward was going on in that household. "People who drink at home, are not necessarily drunkards," he had said, "all the drunkards seen in the Armenian quarters in the evening are those who aren't permitted to drink at home. They are not Armenians. Do you ever see drunken Armenians in the street? No, of course you don't, because they are allowed to drink at home." Interesting reasoning, I had allowed, but I wasn't convinced. He must be trying to make me stop worrying about Cousin Tahra, I'd figured.

I had another reason to worry about Father's drinking. Haj Taghi, our wealthy old neighbor was fast losing his mind, and the consensus in Ali Khan Close, the cul-de-sac that defined our cohesive community, was that his past drinking was the cause. Not that he touched the stuff nowadays, having made the sacred pilgrimage to Mecca in Arabia long before my time, which entitled him to prefix his given name Taghi with the honorific *Haj*. Everybody agreed that he was a picture of piety now. And he was determined to show it. He said his prayers on time every day, and publicly. He did his fasting as required, distributed alms, held great gatherings of the faithful in his huge gardens for the purpose of hearing sacred sermons and songs of lamentation for the Martyrs of the Faith. He fed the poor and the jobless on the eve of every Friday, and bought new school uniforms for the neighborhood kids who couldn't afford them. Even Lady Saria, the most pious woman in Ali

Khan Close, and the one with the most exacting criteria in all matters religious, sincerely believed that Haj Taghi's past drinking was already forgiven by the Almighty. But, the fact remained that, before his atonement, he had been seen raising his glass at his Christian friends' Noel parties, and "it was well known," Lady Saria had said more than once, "that there is no known end to calamities that the Devil's brew could cause even long after the last consumption." So I kept worrying about Father's drinking.

It didn't help that Father seemed quite worried himself. His usually shaky hands seemed to be even shakier as the time for the nightly administration of the elixir approached. He attended to the task as strictly and as precisely as he did to his devotional duties. But he looked more and more troubled. As troubled as I was; the prospect of having a drunk father in the house was quite unsettling. Would he, who had never physically punished me except symbolically, now start to behave like Mash Karim and other fathers I knew of, and dispense punishments in earnest for the same infractions that were always treated lightly till now? Would he lose his temper and perhaps his mind? I wished my brother Bagher were in town to shed some light on the situation. I remembered that he was of great help in a similar situation a few years earlier, just days after the occupation of the country by the Soviet Army in 1941: Tabriz was full of Russian soldiers, and the citizens hadn't yet gotten used to the sudden changes in their daily lives, when a neighbor, who was rich and modern enough to own a radio paid us a visit. He seemed to be well-informed on the latest news. "The Russians are rounding up all the *yekabaash* people," he reported. How could he say it so casually? This was such frightening news to me. You see, the word literally meant "large-headed" in the local tongue. Didn't the man notice how large my father's head was? Even a kid could see that. Fortunately, my fears were unfounded. Brother Bagher, seeing me in distress, took me aside and explained to me that in the present context the word only meant very rich or very powerful. To reassure me he gave me an example: a well-known rich man who was already arrested and, if his picture in the newspaper was any indication, his head looked awfully small, especially compared to his abdomen. What a relief!

IT HADN'T BEEN EASY FOR FATHER to accept the medical advice about the forbidden drink. He had finally agreed to take the medicine, but only after consultations with four "physicians." The first in the sequence—determined in the increasing order of their fees—didn't even claim to be a doctor and was only licensed to give injections ordered by licensed doctors. But he had an office nearby, where he also recommended and sold nonprescription drugs. Father thought we should give him some business. So for common complaints we always went to him first. The cure for Father's current ailment, however, wasn't in this man's repertory; so, he humbly suggested that Father consult experts of higher order.

Then there was the unforgettable Hajmirzali, the unlicensed, self-educated physician-philosopher, who entertained clients at home, not too far from Ali Khan Close. He was inexpensive and convenient, but Father, for some reason, didn't have as much confidence in his medical expertise as he did in his religious rectitude. While I write this account now, more than seventy years later, I vividly remember this colorful medicine-man from my single encounter with him.

I must have been about ten years old (perhaps a year after the cognac saga I am now digressing from). A female neighbor had taken ill suddenly one afternoon. So when I arrived back from school, I was hastily dispatched to serve as her obligatory male chaperon to visit Hajmirzali's establishment. As in many old, traditional homes of the well-to-do in Tabriz, the main entrance opened to a *dalan*—a small and rather dark enclosure with two separate doors inside it. One led to his inner courtyard and family quarters which in his case, as I would learn later, housed his three or four wives and his uncountable offspring. This door was of course closed when my charge and I entered the dalan. The second door, open to us now, led to a compact outer courtyard with a sizable room on one side and an outhouse on the other. There was also a small pool in the middle of the yard and, next to it, an aftafa to be filled and carried to the outhouse as need arose. This provided for visitors' required ablutions and made it unnecessary for them to enter the inner sanctum in search of the needed facilities. Hajmirzali's outer room, originally designed to entertain male guests in a household of this sort, now served as his medical office as well.

Once my charge and I arrived in the office, I knew that this wasn't an ordinary, dull, sometimes scary, doctor's office at all. The impressive figure of the *hakim*—the term had originally meant a wise man or a philosopher, but it was now used in everyday language to refer to a physician, especially

an unlicensed one, who couldn't be legally called a doctor—
sat majestically at the far end of the room we now entered.
There was a thick carpet on the floor for the patients to
sit on, with a few divans for more important visitors. The
hakim's own throne consisted of an extra-thick cushion and
two cylindrical pillows supporting his back. His complexion
was very fair and his beard very black. He was wearing a
flat "house hat" and a comfortable robe, like my father's.
He looked to me like an old clergyman without a turban,
but he couldn't have been very old. (Otherwise, his beard
would have been white or at least grey, unless he dyed it
with henna, in which case it would have been orange-red.)
Around the room on the floor and along the four walls were
seated many, perhaps as many as a dozen, female patients
together with their respective boy-chaperons. This was
no doubt a time slot designated for women. The ladies all
appeared old or middle-aged from beneath their all-em-
bracing black *charshubs*. The accompanying boys all seemed
to be about my age.

There was a large bronze mortar in front of Hakim
Hajmirzali. Surrounding the mortar were several shallow
ceramic bowls containing substances of varying shapes
and colors. Some were obviously dried herbs, some looked
like crushed seeds or nuts. The hakim had a pestle in his
right hand and seemed to be gently pounding and mixing
whatever was in the mortar, piously holding his gaze down
on account of the female presence. To indicate that it was a
particular woman's turn for consultation, he simply used his
left hand to point to the boy accompanying the woman. The
pair then moved closer to him, and the patient informed the

hakim of her complaints. Both the hakim and the patient kept looking down, both addressed the boy instead of each other directly. Only the people nearest them heard their conversation. But we all noticed the brief reflective pause on the part of the hakim followed by the preparation of the prescribed remedy: Hajmirzali's left hand reached a couple of the medicine bowls, grabbed some of the contents from each, and added it to what was already in the mortar. His right hand with the pestle did some more pounding and stirring, after which his left hand picked a large sheet of newsprint from a thick stack placed under the cushion he was sitting on. He then wrapped most of the contents of the mortar in the sheet and handed it to the boy-chaperon and gave instructions on how much of the concoction should be used each time, and how often. The well-crushed remnant in the mortar was then saved as a base for the medication to be prescribed to the next patient in line.

THIS FIRST-HAND EXPERIENCE with Hajmirzali's medical practice was still in the future for me, of course, when the hakim was briefly considered by Father, in the sequence of physicians, and then skipped for the time being. The situation was serious enough for Father to go directly to the third authority on his unwritten list. Dr. Hamid Khan was actually licensed to use the title of "Doctor" on the sign he proudly displayed on his door, although he had not gone to a regular medical school. Like his father and grand-father before him, he had learned the skills at his father's knee. He was sufficiently competent to pass the licensing examination conducted by the newly established Ministry of Health. Now that there was a modern medical school in the capital city, the Central Government was determined to weed out those it called unqualified practitioners, mainly the adherents of traditional strictly herbal solutions. Dr. Hamid Khan was famous for combining traditional and modern methods. Two of his favorite remedies, "wind extraction" and bloodletting by leeches, were tried on Father first. But I must explain.

Recommended when "harmful winds" were detected, trapped somehow and somewhere under the skin of a patient, the extraction method was the most amusing medical procedure to me—unlike the bloodletting method which I found scary. I even participated in the extraction operation: Mother strategically positioned a candle butt, or a small kerosene-daubed rag on Father's horizontal, bare back. I got ready for my part, carefully holding a clear tea-glass in my hands, upside down. Mother then lit the little "lamp," and trusted me with placing the glass firmly over it fast enough to prevent skin burns. Then I watched with fascination how the flame disappeared, how the glass was filled with smoke, and how through the smoke I then managed to see the targeted area of Father's body swelling. When I was allowed to remove the glass, which required applying considerable force on my part, I witnessed the temporary mound on Father's back gradually returning to its normal level. I assumed naturally that the unwanted winds had thus been expelled—smoked out, to use a term that would become popular with certain world leaders sixty years later, when referring to successful military operations in the Middle East. The procedure was of course repeated as many times as the volume of the hidden evil winds, estimated by Dr. Hamid Khan, required.

These methods, together with herbal remedies, didn't seem to be working. That is how Dr. Hamid Khan came up with this cognac prescription that shocked us all. Father's knowledge of the tenets of the Faith was quite extensive; so he knew that there *were* certain rare and desperate situations in which a God-fearing doctor could prescribe an alcoholic remedy to a God-fearing patient, as a last resort. But he wasn't at all sure that this was such a situation. He had always made fun of an old business colleague of his who was known to drink wine and claim that it was under his doctor's orders. "His doctor's faith is as suspect as his, if not more," Father had said. "The man is never sober long enough for him or his doctor to find out if the wine had any real effect." Now there was little reason to doubt Dr. Hamid Khan's piety, but Father wanted to be positive about the absolute necessity of the prescription. For preliminary steps, he decided to get a second and a third opinion. He first turned to Hakim Hajmirzali, whose adherence to sacred principals was unimpeachable. The hakim, trusting Father's piety in turn, concurred. He wasn't even cross with Father for not coming to him first; perhaps because he had never himself ventured to prescribe unholy medicines. Next, Father made a visit to Dr. Herand, the most highly educated (in Paris, France, if I can trust my memory) and the most respected practitioner on our family's list. Dr. Herand did not share our faith, but Father said he is a staunch follower of his own Christian faith and could be trusted to be as careful in these matters as any doctor could be. A visit to him more than confirmed Dr. Hamid Khan's opinion, except that Dr. Herand seemed to be recommending a higher dose of the unusual medicine. Anyway, everything that could be done about medical consultations was now done.

But Father wasn't quite ready yet to act on the unusual prescription. There was one more thing he decided he should do, a further step which he never took lightly: something tantamount to consulting the Almighty Himself. The normal procedure for this holy consultation was familiar to me: It would be preceded by requisite ablutions and prayers performed by the supplicant, who would then pick the Holy Book with utmost care and respect, and open it to what looked like a random page to the uninitiated eye. The interpretation of the verses now in view would result in a recommendation that could range from strongly positive to emphatically negative. Laymen and laywomen usually asked a trustworthy clergyman to perform this service, but Father was more scripturally learned than the average man of cloth and quite confident that he could manage it himself. In fact, he had done it for other people before (and was always extremely annoyed by those who dared to ask him to repeat it when the verdict from Heaven wasn't to their liking). Whether it was for a member of his own family, a neighbor, or a friend, Father performed this service only in connection with pending decisions of great potential consequences such as a marriage proposal or a home purchase. (When my eldest brother had been half-promised a government scholarship to study in France, for instance, a solemn consultation on the advisability of such a momentous journey was called for. Father performed it, and the result was lukewarm. Thus he did not share my brother's deep feelings of disappointment when the Ministry of Education had a change of mind about the scholarship.)

The present occasion was of course momentous enough to warrant a consultation with the Highest Authority. Father performed the ablutions and did the ritual praying and advice-seeking. And, to Mother's great relief, the outcome was very favorable. Obeying the doctors' orders was at last approved from above and Father's reluctance duly controlled.

Now cognac couldn't be purchased like an ordinary drug from a pharmacy, and there was no prescription to present to a purveyor anyway. The problem Father was facing was not trivial. "Who is going to put the bell-collar on the cat now?" Father asked, proving that he hadn't lost all sense of humor after the very long, strenuous decision-making process. He was quoting from a variant of the famous Persian fable, "Mouse and Cat," famously told in verse by the fourteenth-century satirist Obayd Zakani. In this version, a community of mice get together and decide to put an end to the atrocities of the powerful, ruthless, and corrupt cat. Having exhausted all peaceful methods of negotiating with the enemy, they finally come up with the ingenious idea of a bellcollar to be put on the cat which would warn them of the tyrant's comings and goings. When they have procured a suitable bellcollar with great effort and expense, however, they have to face the big question—the one now being asked by Father, not totally in jest: Who is to put the bell collar on the cat's neck?

Father wouldn't be caught dead inside any of the few stores in Tabriz which sold alcoholic beverages. He would certainly not send me to such a store, and would be too embarrassed to ask a friend for the favor. Mother wouldn't even want to be seen in the vicinity of those stores. Brother Bagher, Father assumed, had connections and could obtain the unorthodox medicine discreetly, but he was out of town. So we waited. When Bagher returned, it took him only a couple of hours to bring home the prescribed potion in a grey bottle—acquired, he said, through an Armenian acquaintance. Thus began Father's grudging but very exact observance of doctors' orders: one tablespoonful of the fluid in his after-dinner cup of tea, every evening at the same precise time. To him this was the most potent drug he had ever taken. And he expected fast, unmistakable results to make it worth the guilt, the worry, and the inconvenience.

After a week or so no immediate improvement in Father's condition was observed. So Mother took her cousin Tahra, the one with the traveling-salesman husband, into her confidence. "He doesn't seem to be getting any results," Mother said to her visiting cousin over a cup of tea at the cozy kursi one afternoon, before Father's habitual time of arrival at home. (My parents never referred to each other by their first names. For Mother it was "the children's father" on formal occasions, but just "he" otherwise. For Father it almost always seemed to be "the home"—as in "Heydar, run home and tell the home we'll have company for dinner tonight; three guests.") Tahra was surprised that Father's doctor would prescribe such minute amounts of this particular medicine. Her "he" was apparently getting great results, but from glassfuls, not spoonfuls. This conversation, which was certainly not to be reported to Father, only diminished Mother's respect for Tahra's husband's doctor. It also, thank God, largely reduced my fear of the possible delayed effects which the contents of the grey bottle might have on Father's sobriety and mental health. After all, Cousin Tahra's husband was still capable of functioning as a sober, sane, upright citizen of Tabriz.

Father was becoming more and more impatient with the lack of spectacular results expected from the offensive medicine. "Maybe you should see Dr. Hamid Khan again," Mother suggested meekly after three or four weeks. "Perhaps a larger dose is needed as Dr. Herand suggested." Father's view on the subject was firm and clear. "Medicine is not food," he reminded Mother. "It is too potent for liberal or prolonged use, and one should not allow one's body to get addicted to it. Were this remedy effective at all, we would have seen some clear results by now." While still adhering religiously, but more reluctantly, to the doctor's instructions, he started a careful reading of the relevant chapters of his valued, all-purpose, reference book, *The Modicum*, on the subject of fatigue. (The full title of the book was, in my free translation, "A Modicum of What Everybody Needs to Know in Everyday Living.")

SPRING WAS APPROACHING, and with it Father's annual period of gardening activities. A few ounces of the liquid was still left in the cognac bottle. Father came home one evening with a large container full of honey and a sizable paper bag full of powdered ginger. Mother, knowing that we were not short of either item yet, assumed naturally that he had located an inexpensive grocery. "I should have trusted the Modicum more than the doctors," he said, adding that he had decided to give a try to the ultra-large doses of honey-and-ginger remedy presented in that book. The reason he hadn't done so before, he explained, was that the recommended dosage had sounded so excessive. But surely, resorting to extra-ordinary cognac treatment was far more excessive in retrospect. He would start the new treatment immediately: he would dissolve three tablespoons of honey and two teaspoons of ground ginger in his tea twice a day.

That evening Father had his first cup of the new, uncontaminated, alternative potion. He took a contemptuous look at the almost-empty cognac bottle still sitting in the far high shelf. "I shouldn't have started it at all," he said. "I should have known better." Mother reminded him that he'd done so after consulting the Almighty, and the answer was affirmative. "Yes," he agreed, "but my question was about the advisability of a normally forbidden remedy as a last resort. This was obviously not a case of last resort." As soon as the new treatment was repeated the next morning after breakfast, he walked toward the evil bottle with obvious contempt and determination. He grabbed it and carried it to the outhouse on the far side of the courtyard. He seemed full of new-found energy. He called me, after he had disposed of the content, to help him with the task of washing and cleansing the bottle in the proper manner required of pious adherents of the Faith.

As we placed the empty, clean bottle on the basement shelf to be used in summertime for preserving fruit juice,

I could clearly see the expected miracle unfolding: Father already looked unworried, victorious and, yes, healthy. "You'll help me get our flower seeds ready to plant soon," he said to me, while he took a long, loving look at the still wintry backyard. He was confident that the new honey-and-ginger regimen will, by the coming spring, render him equal to his annual gardening tasks.

Look to Your Left First

"Hey! Beware of the donkeys, Son!" I heard a man shout at me urgently. It was this grandfatherly figure, clearly a farmer herding his four or five donkeys, all heavily laden with fresh fruit, and fast approaching me. I was on my way to school, sharing the narrow street with him and his charges. "Why are you looking the wrong way, Son?" he asked me in reproach, when he got my attention. Then he yelled again, as hard as he could this time: "Get out of the way, quick!" Warned just in time, I stepped back and squeezed my body into an alcove in the mud-and-straw wall. The alcove, very typical of traditional entrances to Tabriz homes, especially those built before the mid-twentieth century, allowed the doorway to be set back a step or two from the road. As soon as I was safely in the alcove, the donkeys trotted by, followed by the farmer himself. The old man was still viewing me with a puzzled expression: What was this grown boy—I was nine years old—who ought to know better, doing, looking away from the approaching danger? It wasn't that I was an inexperienced walker. I had crossed the same street every day on my way to and from school for more than two years already, with no difficulty at all. Until now. What caused the problem this time was my intention to experiment with a mysterious method of street crossing: I had just encountered this new recipe for road crossing in the new second-grade reader. But I must explain.

I was in the third grade of elementary school. We were still using old editions of school textbooks. The Ministry of Education had, several years earlier, undertaken a radical program of textbook modernization whose implementation wouldn't catch up with me for another year. At this point, only first- and second-grade pupils were supplied with the fancy new books in shiny covers. I saw the modern second-grade reader in my younger friend Mamadali's possession and was immediately fascinated by it. It had no resemblance to the old Persian readers that I, or my older brother a dozen years before me, or my oldest brother a dozen years before *him*, had used. Uniform textbooks had always been issued by the Ministry of Education for the whole nation, and they hadn't changed much in the two decades preceding my school years. In fact, just the year before, I had been able to recycle an older cousin's fifteen-year-old copy of the Persian reader for second grade, which he had succeeded in keeping clean all this time. Only a handful of pages were different from my classmates' copies of the most recent edition. To render the book usable, my father and I carefully made exact replicas of the up-to-date pages by hand and pasted them over the outdated ones. One of the old pages that I particularly remember was the one containing the statement "Our King is His Majesty Reza Shah Pahlavi," which was no longer true after the occupation of the country by the Allies in World War II, resulting in the monarch's exile to Johannesburg.

I couldn't get over how totally different Mamadali's textbook was from mine, in form as well as in content. Not one page of it matched my own second-grade book from the previous year. Nobody, I figured, would ever again be able to recycle any textbook printed before 1940. The old-style Persian readers, including the third-grade book I was currently using in school—evidently for the last time in the history of elementary education—had been lithographed, not typeset. This allowed for ample displays of best samples of Persian calligraphy, a most important art form in Iran. The old textbooks also contained centuries-old, didactic tales and fables chosen from well-known Persian works of prose and verse. The students were always responsible for the inevitable question, "What lessons do we learn from this story?" So every such item came with at least one discernible, and quite predictable, moral. But the modernized second-grade reader which I, snuggled under the warm *kursi* in Mamadali's living room on this cold winter afternoon, was now holding in my hands was unrecognizably different. It was typeset, just like newspapers, only in larger type. And this was just the beginning. With its illustrations of fashionably dressed kids and their parents, with its numerous puzzles and word games, and with its funny stories written specifically for children, it looked more like a magazine than a proper textbook. I was sure my septuagenarian father would find it not only too frivolous for a school text, but also detrimental to school kids' handwriting skills.

Forever suspicious of all government policies and hidden intentions behind them, Father had reservations even about the old editions. "They are just preparing you for your compulsory military service," he had said on more than one occasion. So I wasn't surprised by his reaction when I showed him a passage in my textbook on the importance of daily exercise for people of all ages. "As far as civilians are concerned," he asserted, shaking his head, "playing outdoors is sufficient exercise for kids. So is doing the necessary daily chores for adults." What would he say now, I tried to imagine, if he were to see Mamadali's Persian reader with all the children's stories? All the pictures of mothers with bare hair, just like those in foreign magazines? Drawings of all the boys and girls playing in shorts and T-shirts? Mamadali's grandmother Lady Saria's potential objections to the new, frivolous textbooks were to be feared even more—compared to her, Father was quite lenient. She didn't like the pictures at all. She didn't even like the names of the little male and female characters in the book: Gone were most of the Biblical and Quranic names and those of the great Martyrs of the Faith. Almost all the little boys and girls featured in this new textbook seemed to have been given pure Persian names from the nation's mythological past.

I cannot quite trust my memory here, but I am pretty sure that seeing Mamadali's sinfully illustrated new reader played a part in Lady Saria's drastic action to follow soon after: All of a sudden she would take Mamadali out of the "modern" school he was attending together with me and, oblivious to Mamadali's young father's opinion on the matter—his young mother had already been divorced on Lady Saria's orders, for not being sufficiently obedient to her—would register him in a religious school: One of those old-fashioned elementary schools for boys, the kind my father had attended in the 1870s. They had resurfaced now that the sworn enemy of such schools in the person of Reza

Shah the Modernizer was gone. Everything in Mamadali's alternative school seemed to be to Lady Saria's liking. The pupils dutifully sat on the floor of the one-room school forming a circle, just as their ancestors had done dozens of generations before, and their hearts and minds were properly filled with fear of God and teacher. (The aged teacher, Mamadali would confide in me later, owned a stick long enough to reach every seated pupil in the school room. Thus the parties involved in the very frequent acts of punishment, an essential part of the alternative schooling, did not have to move at all from where they were sitting, or even lift a limb except the right arm of the master and the two hands of the pupil to be punished. The little hands were opened and held up conveniently together at chest level, one supporting the other, ready to be struck.)

Mamadali's new textbook, soon to be abandoned, thanks to Lady Saria's new plans for her grandson's education, could have come from another planet. Particularly disliked by the lady were the book's depictions of what she took to be mixed company, sitting in chairs around a dinner table. In her household there was of course no such table. Everybody kneeled around a table-cloth, spread on the carpeted floor, to eat. And if they had mixed company, separate table cloths in separate rooms were required. In my household, as in most of my neighbors' in Ali Khan Close at the time, we used chairs and tables only when we were entertaining formal guests—separating genders, of course.

Another illustration in this textbook, also abhorred by Lady Saria, showed well-dressed women and men strolling together in groups, and pushing baby carriages in the park. None of the mothers in our neighborhood pushed a baby carriage in the park or strolled together with a man. Mamadali and I viewed the pictures with amusement and envy. We pretended to be the strolling parents in the pictures. To look like them, we used handkerchiefs for neckties, straw wastebaskets for hats, and rolled-up paper for cigarettes. Most aspects of the awe-inspiring lives the inhabitants of the new book seemed to lead were not so mysterious to us kids as they were inaccessible.

But I did find one item utterly incomprehensible in the new textbook: It was this method of street crossing, this puzzling recipe I have already mentioned. Not that the directions were hard to follow. I remember them well: "To cross a street," it instructed us, "look first to the left, walk half way across, stop momentarily, then look to the right before proceeding to the other side." I decided to ask a knowledgeable grownup for an explanation later, but for now I was fascinated by the instructions. It was uncanny. It almost sounded like the familiar dictum regulating pre-ablutionary behavior of the faithful: "When entering a washroom, set your left foot in first." Was this also a kind of imported religious directive then, this weird method of street crossing? But I readily rejected this hypothesis; it just wasn't consistent with the other contents of the book.

No matter how I looked at it, the advice just didn't make sense. My mother had told me, almost every day during my first year in school, that I should look both ways before crossing. And it had worked well for me so far. The narrow street leading from the "mouth" of our cul-de-sac, Ali Khan Close, to my school was a typical Tabriz street of the day, except for a very few relatively wide avenues constructed recently. Part of my path to school was a *bazaarcha*, a small covered market, with shops on both sides, where we did our daily food shopping. This section was free of animals except for delivery donkeys in the early part of the day. No other means of transportation was allowed in the bazaarcha. The uncovered, residential part of my path was the "dangerous part," and Mother repeatedly instructed me to be extra careful when negotiating it. "Don't talk to passersby, don't play, don't read, don't stare at the clouds, don't fall asleep, beware of the traffic, watch the ground for holes while you cross the street." The nonhuman traffic consisted mainly of donkeys, mules, and horse-drawn *arabas* transporting goods. And a few *doroshkehs* serving as cabs for hire. No buses could fit into our street. In all my first two years in elementary school, I saw only one car in this street. Its well-dressed and very angry driver had risked traveling on the rough cobblestone surface of this road and gotten stuck in the middle, providing great amusement for us cruel kids. Not that there were many cars in the city anyway. The only motor vehicles capable of negotiating our neighborhood seemed to be those belonging to the occupying Red Army, but luckily for us pedestrians, they were forced by the road conditions to move much more slowly than we the pedestrians or the donkeys did.

THIS IS HOW IT CAME ABOUT THAT, having read the instructions in my friend's modern textbook, and having decided to give it a tentative try, I was looking to the left first before crossing. That was when, alarmed by the old farmer's yelling from the right, I escaped serious injury which his trotting charges could cause. Scared and regretful of the attempted application of a dubious and unfamiliar crossing technique, but still very curious, I decided to halt my experimentation and to educate myself further on the matter.

"I have never heard of such a thing," said Mother when I arrived home and casually mentioned the curious, modern method of street crossing I had learned from the new textbook. "I don't know what they are talking about, but please, please, no new tricks! Do me a favor; don't be lazy; promise me you'll look both ways when crossing. Always." I didn't want to scare her. I didn't tell her about the trotting donkeys whose operator I had just puzzled and annoyed. Mamadali was also curious about the method, but he postponed experimenting with it, and we didn't dare talk about it to Lady Saria. She would probably link it to yet another scheming plot by the foreign infidels to reduce the population of true believers. To think of it now, I am sure that my father would have had a satisfactory answer— having seen in his youth a bit of the outside world. But at the time I was hesitant to ask him. What if he didn't know? I wondered. I was afraid of embarrassing him. (The fear was probably not justified: was he embarrassed when I asked him about the modern methods of adding and subtracting on paper that I was learning in school, as opposed to his customary way of doing all his calculations with an abacus?) To avoid embarrassing myself, I didn't ask my teacher either; after all, this was apparently material to be learned and talked about in a lower grade than mine. I decided to wait for my older brother, Bagher, due to arrive back from Tehran soon. I was positive he would know the answer.

"There is only one possibility in the whole city of Tabriz," said Bagher once I had the opportunity to bring up the subject. "Only one road where this rule could even make sense, maybe." He was talking about Pahlavi Avenue, which at the time looked to me incredibly, and unnecessarily, wide. It had dividers in the middle to force the traffic in either direction to stay in their half. As in almost every town in Iran, this avenue, being the main thoroughfare in Tabriz, was named after the king—and to accommodate the politics of changing times, it would later be officially renamed again and again. For now, it was the only paved road in town; so everybody I knew called it simply "the Paved Avenue." Perhaps they knew from experience that official names were too transient. The unofficial, politically neutral, name stuck, until there were more paved avenues.

The Paved Avenue and the city park right on it consti-tuted the modern center of the city, the place to see, and to be seen in, if you had any claims to being "with it." You could take a stroll there or have an ice cream bar at one of the concessions along its sidewalks. The Paved Avenue was lined with expensive shops which sold the kind of goods featured in Mamadali's new second-grade reader: baby carriages, dining tables and chairs, radio sets, phone sets, electric fans and vacuum cleaners, even toy cars for kids. The fancier stores had huge signs that mentioned, among other things, their telephone numbers, each in four proud digits. "Why the number?" I asked my brother once, "What do you do with it?" I knew only one rich relative whose house was equipped with the prestigious item and I had actually observed him in the enviable act of making a phone call: he simply called the phone center in Tabriz, gave the operator the name of another lucky phone owner in the city, and requested a connection. I saw no need for the *number* of the phone you had the privilege of owning or using. "Nobody needs the number of a phone in Tabriz," agreed Brother Bagher, giving me a familiar cynical smile combined with an arched eyebrow, "but how else can they advertise the fact that they are prosperous enough to afford a telephone?"

The Paved Avenue also seemed to have accommodated the offices of most of the city's important doctors who were obviously not shy about listing their credentials on huge, eye-catching signs affixed to the wall above their office doors. "Dr. M. Karimnejad, General Surgeon," would announce a typical, colorfully calligraphed sign. "The Holder of a Doctorate from Paris" would be the coveted and preferred phrase to follow the name and title on the sign. Otherwise, "the Former Resident of Paris Hospitals" would have to do. "Resident" was of course spelled in Persian, something sounding like "rezeedaan," a transliteration of the French "*résident.*" I wanted to know what the word meant. "It is supposed to mean," explained my brother, "that the good doctor probably got his doctoral degree at home, but extended his knowledge and experience by working and performing surgery in Paris hospitals." He told me the literal meaning of the French word, and then added, "But who knows, some people say the guy just 'resided' for a while in a rented room near a hospital in Paris."

All the three movie theaters of Tabriz were, naturally, located on or just off the fancy Paved Avenue. So were, according to my recollection, the only two modern buildings in the city that were more than three stories high. So also were the two chic food stores that sold such things as Dutch cheeses and cognac; and the only bookstore that sold books in Western languages. (The numerous traditional bookstores of Tabriz were mostly concentrated in one locality in the great bazaar area that was, oddly enough, called "The Glaziers' Market.") The only full modern high school of Tabriz at the time, the awe-inspiring Ferdowsi High School, of which my brothers were proud graduates, and which I was destined to attend in a few years' time, also stood on the Paved Avenue. It was here on this avenue, as well, that you could catch an occasional glimpse of the "beautiful people" of Tabriz, that select group of citizens who were called *Frangi-ma'ab* by the people outside the group. (The hyphenated designation had to wait a few decades for an accurate translation into English; that is, until certain two words came together to form a single word: the term could at last be interpreted as "one with French lifestyle.") It was an eye-opener to see Frangi-ma'ab individuals in person, and not just in the pictures of Mamadali's textbook. How different these men, women, and children were from those I saw every day in our local bazaarcha!

Frangi-ma'ab women of the Paved Avenue appeared in public with uncovered faces and heads, walking not behind but alongside their male companions. Their men wore well-pressed suits, shiny laced shoes, and colorful neckties. Those inhabitants of Tabriz who did not consider it sinful for women to leave home with exposed hair formed a very tiny minority, of course. Even tinier was the minority of those who dared to practice what they believed. They were indeed very daring, given the circumstances. After all, they were no longer subjected to the rules enforced by the formidable former Shah's emancipation police. Instead, they now faced tremendous pressures in the opposite direction coming from the recently energized pious traditionalists. So few were the uncovered female faces in the street now that everybody seemed to know the full names of the individuals to whom the faces belonged. "How did you like the new orange outfit on Susan Heshmati?" I would overhear a strolling young man asking a male companion, as if they had just left a dinner party together after saying farewell to Susan Heshmati. In reality, they had only been feasting their eyes on her beautiful form promenading along the Paved Avenue. "Not bad," would come the answer, "but she would be truly dazzling in pink, I'd say." The cruel law of supply and demand would often result in simultaneous crushes on one Susan Heshmati or another by a hundred teenage boys, as my personal experience would attest in a few years' time. For now I compared all the Susans I encountered on the sidewalks of the Paved Avenue to the pictures of pretty movie stars adorning the walls of my little room, cut out of foreign magazines and pasted there several years earlier by my brother Bagher, a teenager at the time. I would learn later why it was prudent on Bagher's part to put his girlie pictures on my walls rather than his: Father wouldn't have approved of those decorations on Bagher's own walls. *My* walls were safe for the time being. They were not subject to paternal censure as long as I was still considered an innocent kid. When able to pick Hedy Lamarr from among the pictures on my wall and recognize her beautiful face, I too would have to remove all inappropriate female images from my walls, Hedy Lamarr included.

I wasn't yet permitted to go to the dangerously wide Paved Avenue by myself. On those rare weekend occasions when Brother Bagher took me there, he consistently held my hand when crossing. Thus I had felt safe and allowed myself to be absorbed in the exotic sights and sounds of the avenue, paying no attention to the opposing directions of traffic. When Bagher explained the logic behind the crossing recipe for pedestrians that had so mystified me, I was delighted with this clever method, and wanted to try it where it was surely applicable, possible, and safe—on the Paved Avenue. "You will do no such thing!" my brother admonished me once he heard of my plan, "Do you think all drivers know the rules?" I wasn't dissuaded, though, until the next time he took me to the Paved Avenue. Then I paid more attention to the traffic and noticed that even there the method wouldn't work perfectly: The only tram rails of Tabriz, connecting the center of the city to the railway station, ran on one and the same side of the Paved Avenue. But the direction of the horse-drawn trams had to keep changing back and forth, of course.

"DOES EVERYBODY IN FRANCE always stick to the right side of the road?" I asked Jalal Khan, a business associate of my father's, whose son had been to Paris and who never tired of describing the glories of everyday life in Europe.

"How do they train their donkeys and horses to observe the rules?" I wanted to know, "Do they have tram rails on both sides of their streets? Are all their streets wide enough?" My father had warned me about Jalal Khan's exaggerated expressions of his long-distance love for Paris, a city the man had never visited himself. "You can believe only every other word he says about Europe," Father had told me, and he was right. "Take, for example," Father had reminded me, "what Jalal Khan once said about the sidewalks of the Avenue des Champs-Elysées being entirely tiled with little mirrors."

Yes, and I also remembered the colorful Jalal Khan going on and on about how honest, civilized, observant, knowledgeable, and punctual everybody in Europe, especially in Switzerland, was. A friend of his had, it seemed, been to Geneva. "My friend swears to God," Jalal Khan once reported, "that just to test the citizens of Geneva personally, he placed his own pocket watch near a wall on a sidewalk and, would you believe it? That same evening the watch was returned to him by the police, who brought it directly to his hotel." "But how did the police know it belonged to him?" asked an amazed member of Jalal Khan's audience. "I was puzzled also," confessed Jalal Khan, "and so was my friend himself, understandably. So he had to get to the bottom of it all. His watch was Swiss, of course. Now it so happens that the Swiss watch manufacturers can tell, by a code etched on every watch, which country it was exported to. There aren't too many Iranians in Geneva, you know; so, as soon as an honest citizen rushed the watch to the nearest police station, the clerks knew what to do: They matched the code on the watch with the list of registrants in every hotel in

Geneva. This list is always at their disposal, together with all the relevant information, including their countries of origin. This is how the police found the names and whereabouts of all the Iranians in Geneva. Thus my friend was reunited with his watch within a couple of hours." So, of course I had misgivings about Jalal Khan's seemingly limitless knowledge about what he called "the truly civilized world." Yet, he was one of the very few people I knew who had claims to recent connections to Europe, and I hoped that his answers to the simple questions I'd just put to him, wouldn't be dispensed with undue exaggeration.

"To start with," said Jalal Khan, evidently appreciative of the opportunity to enlighten me on the subject of traffic in *Frangistan*, "let me tell you that in the clean streets of Paris, they don't have all these dirty donkeys, mules, and their illiterate herders roaming about. This is all illegal in Frangistan. There, every means of transportation is motorized and driven by the people who can read and understand traffic signs. And, yes, every one of them sticks to the right side of the road, and yes, all avenues in France and in all the other modernized countries are wide enough to have sidewalks and often two lanes in each direction, one for trams and another for cars and buses." But Jalal Khan offered more than just answers to my questions. "I also understand," he added, "that they now have automatic traffic lights powered by electricity, which have actually replaced policemen standing at busy intersections, to direct the traffic. The lights change from color to color: green means go, red means stop, and so on." I decided to believe him on this one. I imagined an automatic light in the middle of my narrow path to school, a miraculous light that knew when it was safe for donkeys to proceed and when it was not. Wow! I thought, this was the magic of science my Uncle Hussen kept talking about.

SIXTY-ONE YEARS LATER, on a return visit to Tabriz, I sat in the cell-phone shop on the Paved Avenue. The shop belonged to Mehdi, my late brother Bagher's son. I was waiting for my nephew to come and take me to see a relative. I started to read a newspaper, but it was hard to concentrate. The onslaught of the Paved Avenue memories was irresistible. The official name of the avenue had, in the meantime, changed three times. First in the mid-forties, from Pahlavi to Sattar Khan—after the revered hero of the 1906 Constitutional Revolution. Then back to Pahlavi, the Shah's last name. And most recently to Imam Khomeini—after the leader of the 1979 Revolution. But a lot more than the name had changed. Looking out of the store window, I spotted a flashing traffic light and remembered my fascination with the tale of the magical, automatic traffic lights in Paris.

I remembered Jalal Khan. I remembered how, after Jalal Khan mentioned those Parisian devices, I had been waiting to see one installed in Tabriz. Sure enough, one such light appeared on our Paved Avenue a few years later, not long after I enrolled in my beloved Ferdowsi High School on that Avenue. I remembered also that by then the tram lines had been removed. So, the look-to-your-left-first rule had, for a few decades, become applicable to crossings. Not just on the original Paved Avenue, but on some other newly-constructed wide and paved roads as well. Most of the citizenry understood how the rule worked and how the traffic light operated. But older people still considered the lights useless imported toys, and made fun of the seemingly arbitrary color changes. Enough drivers, young and old, ignored it so that a policeman had to be stationed next to each of the traffic lights at busy intersections to holler at them and occasionally fine them. (Long after quite a few of these gadgets had been installed everywhere in Iran and every city dweller was finally familiar with their operation, an Iranian fellow student of mine at the University of Minnesota bragged to me about fooling the traffic police in Minneapolis. He claimed that, upon being caught driving through a red light, he had played dumb and said to the questioning police officer, "Sorry, but in my country it is the other way around, Officer; we stop on green and proceed on red." To make his story more believable, he had added, he said, "As you know, Officer, we also write from right to left, instead of the other way around." The officer wasn't surprised, the rascal reported, and let him go unticketed, but warned him sternly, "Remember, in this country we have different rules." I had no reason to doubt him then, and sitting in my nephew's shop and reminiscing fondly about the innocent Minnesota of my student days in the late 1950s, I had no reason to doubt him now.)

I knew, of course, that "the Paved Avenue" had long ceased to be an unambiguous address, because there was practically no unpaved road or street in Tabriz now. This morning, after giving up on my initial idea of walking to Mehdi's store, on account of high air pollution, I had given the current official name of the Paved Avenue to the driver of the cab I took. He struggled through the now permanently traffic-jammed streets to get me to my nephew's store. The driver was, evidently, still loyal to the memory of the *ancient régime*: he refused to use the new name of the road and kept referring to it as "the former Pahlavi Avenue." (One hard-core secular socialist, an old-timer I met the day before, obviously disliked both of the last two regimes. He went another step back and kept referring to it as Sattar Khan Avenue.) Every major intersection, as far as I could tell, was now equipped with an automatic traffic light. But they were all utterly useless: Overpopulation and vehicle congestion, combined with the impatience of drivers, had forced the authorities to put every single one of the lights in perpetual flashing mode. This gave drivers the satisfaction of not having to stop unnecessarily. But it also made it seem impossible for pedestrians to cross a busy street—unless they were, unlike me, well-tutored in the art of making simultaneous eye contact with all the drivers approaching from various directions, and trusting them with their own lives.

The sidewalks on this wide avenue were obviously no longer suitable for the pleasure strolls of yore, and there seemed to be infinitely more men and women rushing about on it than I remembered. Of course, all the women had completely covered their hair and body, some voluntarily and some by the strictures imposed on them by the post-revolutionary Government's morality codes. Similarly, not a single man was in sight sporting a necktie or a Frangi hat. "For a pleasant stroll," said an older man, the proprietor of a neighboring shop who had come for a chat and offered me an apple, "young people nowadays have to go to Vali-Asr

Avenue." He was referring to the new, rather expensive and relatively congestion-free, residential district far from the city center. "Do you mean," I asked, "that there are different rules of conduct there for young people?" "Of course not," he explained, "the morality rules are the same, but they seem a little harder to enforce in the more modern parts of the city." One thing was certain: there were many more girls out now than there had been during my school days. And at least their full faces were now visible to every boy. I figured that the current objects of teenage crushes had substantially tougher competition than the Susan Heshmatis of my day.

Mehdi arrived at his store a little late, having had to park his car far away, on the opposite side of the road. The old neighbor exchanged pleasantries with Mehdi, received due gratitude for having kept his uncle company in his absence, and left. My nephew and I ventured out, made our way through the crowded sidewalk, and approached the roadside, intending to cross and get to his car. The continuous traffic made crossing look like a hellish nightmare to me. I wondered for a moment if the authors of Mamadali's second-grade reader printed in 1942 were now alive and crossing a street in some large city in Iran. Would they still insist on the observance of their own recommended rule on looking to their left first?

"Maybe we should take a cab to the other side," I suggested, and I wasn't just joking. Mehdi gave me a knowing smile, the kind that he had clearly inherited from his father, my bother Bagher. I was too scared to smile back, much more scared to cross now than I had been as a child when Bagher had held my hand to cross the same street, a few blocks away from where we were now standing. My nephew understood. "Give me your hand," he offered, "and shut your eyes, if you wish." He was still smiling. But he sounded quite serious. I took another look at the wide wild river of traffic and decided to rely on Mehdi's hard-earned expertise as a permanent resident of contemporary Tabriz.

As we zigzagged our way to the other side, I was too embarrassed to shut my eyes. But I held his hand as firmly and with as much childlike trust as I had held his father's so long ago.

My Brother's Wind Horse

I was excited to see my older brother Bagher walking a bicycle home. I was also shocked, but let me come back to that in a minute. There had been a time when I would have called the awesome contraption a *yel-aati*, literally meaning a wind horse. But now that I was almost eleven years old, a sophisticated fifth-grader in school, and no longer just one of the many illiterate residents of Ali Khan Close, I knew its correct name.

On this late spring afternoon, I was coming back from school, a couple of hours before Father's expected time of arrival back from work. I couldn't believe my eyes when I caught up with Bagher. Of course, this section of the cul de sac that led to our house at the very end wasn't exactly suited for riding a bike; two people walking abreast could barely pass through this narrowest part of the street with its uneven cobblestone surface. But I knew my brother's real reason for not riding the windhorse. I was really worried, and I knew he was too. What would the pious men and women of Ali Khan Close say if they actually saw him riding a yel-aati? To come to think of it, what were they going to say now, if they saw him just dragging that thing along? What possible use would a respectable household have for this ridiculously oversized toy? I was thinking especially of my neighbor Lady Saria the Pious. And her extreme views on the subject. She had only recently warned her sizable, loyal following in the neighborhood about modern modes of transportation. "I heard from a learned man of God myself," she had said, "who read it in the book of signs, 'Signs of Armageddon,' that toward the end of time, horses and mules will be replaced by strange, evil gadgets." Her audiences had no reason to doubt her or the learned man's quote from the book of signs. Wasn't the reported increase in the number of recent thefts by bikers an indication?

When the excitement of seeing the wondrous machine so close to home had subsided, I was able to concentrate on the first inevitable problem Bagher was to face in a couple of hours. "Does Father know about this?" I asked my brother timidly, certain that Father wouldn't approve of owning or borrowing such an object of frivolity. "It is a business transaction," replied Bagher, with all the authority that his seniority over me by a dozen years entitled him to. "It's second-hand, but in excellent condition. And it was so cheap, I just couldn't pass the opportunity. I am going to sell it for a good profit on my way to Tehran next fall." I was relieved. After all, a bicycle by itself wasn't a forbidden article. Even Father agreed, although I knew Lady Saria wouldn't under any circumstances accept, that the bicycle had its own few legitimate uses. The delivery boy from the Tabriz Telegraph Office, for example, could be said to need one with which to negotiate the narrow alleys of Tabriz. Father would, I hoped, approve of Bagher's business plan. This was very different, I convinced myself, from the questionable practice of a certain young acquaintance, the son of a grocer in the neighborhood, groomed to replace his father upon his retirement, who had recently branched out, disobeying his father in a big way: He had moved to a fashionable part of the city, near Cinema Mayak and opened his own fancy grocery store, where he sold, among other things, a few varieties of *Kalbas*—the word, a corruption of "kielbasa," referred to a variety of polish-style sausage. Now kalbas was known to contain pork, and thus strictly forbidden to the faithful. The young man's excuse was that "this is just business, I carefully keep all my trays of kalbas separate from other foods to avoid contamination, and I only sell it to Christians, who are allowed to eat it, anyway." This was not merely unsatisfactory; it was downright sinful. Sinful enough to cause a complete alienation, for as long afterwards as I remember, between the pious father and the wayward son. Even if my brother dared to ride the bicycle around the city, it would hardly be as bad as handling pork. My father would certainly understand, I tried to assure myself.

BUYING AND SELLING THINGS for a modest profit had always been a favorite pastime with long-distance travelers. The 600-kilometer distance between Tabriz and Tehran was certainly long enough for the practice. The construction of the railroad between the two cities hadn't been completed yet, and no bus or truck could traverse the mostly unpaved, primitive road in less than two full days. Thus every bus on the way to Tehran made a stop in Mianeh or Zanjan for at least one night. In these towns lay the opportunities for the adventurous passenger to conduct some business on the side. As a matter of fact, on his previous trip back from Tehran, my brother had brought a large carpet from Mianeh to sell in Tabriz—an unusual thing to do, as it had seemed to me at first, given that Tabriz was itself a prime exporter of rugs and carpets to every corner of the world. But it was a find, my brother had said, and he couldn't pass the opportunity. I could never forget this adventure of his, because of the big money I'd made as a result of the ensuing transaction that took place right in the courtyard of our house. I even remembered the price at which the rug was eventually sold, because of my astonishing share of the proceeds: a full one percent. As an item for sale by a person other than a professional shop owner in the Great Bazaar, a carpet was substantial enough to require a broker to do the bidding and selling for a ten-percent commission. My brother contacted a carpet broker, who brought in several potential customers. Most of them came while I was the only male in the house to help with the unfolding of the large carpet for viewing and examination; and then refolding and pushing it back to a protected corner of the courtyard. When the right customer finally came and bought the carpet for 140 *tumans*, the broker earned 14 tumans and—how could I ever forget the happy scene of this transaction?—gave me 1.40 tumans, that is 14 *grans*, ten percent of his commission, in recognition of my help. This was 28 times my weekly allowance at the time! Before my tentative plans for spending this windfall had a chance to take shape, however, I was informed by my father that most of the treasure would have to go into my savings account in the Tabriz branch of the National Bank. There it would grow by annual four-percent increments called "prizes" in deference to a dictum of the Faith that forbade paying or receiving any interest on loans or savings. It was quite fair and logical, my elders maintained, that I should be allowed to spend only ten percent of my assistant-broker's cut of the broker's own ten-percent fee.

"Do you need a broker to sell a bicycle?" I now asked my brother, while we walked the bicycle home. I was hoping for another windfall in case he decided to sell it in Tabriz before starting on his travels. "No," he said with an understanding smile, "but I'll give you a small cut when I make a profit. I am not going to sell it in Tabriz anyway; there are better opportunities in small towns on the way." His total dismissal of the possibility of a profitable sale in Tabriz baffled me: wouldn't a sale in town save him the trouble of carrying the bicycle along while he traveled by bus, transferring it from one bus rooftop to another, exposing it to dust, rain, or snow? Was a sale on the road so much more profitable? I wouldn't have an answer for a while.

These dual-purpose trips were common enough to have acquired a colorful, proverbial description, universally understood in both Persian and Turkish: "mixing business with pilgrimage." The term signifies a doubly desirable thing to do—not quite what the English expression it brings to mind, "mixing business with pleasure." The mixing here simply implies that the person engaged in the activity is profiting in two distinct ways: earning a few brownie points for the eternal afterlife by visiting a holy shrine, as well as making a few tumans by conducting a bit of inter-city business for the necessities of the current, transient life on Earth.

A sweet old relative of the family, and a frequent and welcome house guest, Mashammad, who was probably my brother's initial role model in his commercial pursuits, considered himself an accomplished mixer of business with pilgrimage. Every year, he made the holy journey all the way to the shrine in Mashad, the most sacred in the country—1500 kilometers away. (It was his first such trip that entitled him to his current name starting with the honorific "Mash." His original name had been just Mammad. The pilgrimage changed it to Mashadi Mammad, which was shortened to the familiar Mashammad.) Starting his long bus trip from his village near Salmas—our ancestral home town—he always made my house his first stop on the way to Mashad, and his last, a month or so later, when he was returning. He felt blessed to have friends in so many towns on his itinerary, and not just in Tehran, where many members of our extended family now lived. "My friends and relatives are always pleased," he said, "to house a poor old pilgrim for a few days—may God compensate them a thousand-fold for their acts of kindness." It was a given that his hosts got at least a small share of the rewards he was collecting from his holy pilgrimages to be saved for the afterworld. He never forgot to supplement the spiritual earnings of these hosts with small material gifts of his own.

On each of Mashammad's return trips, my mother received from him a small package of saffron, one of the most desirable this-worldly prizes one could get from the holy city of Mashad. My father got brand-new prayer stones, and I got candy. I also received the customary farewell coin on his way out. My brother, too, had fond memories of collecting the sought-after coins from Mashammad's earlier trips, but now that he was a young man, he received a grown-up toy instead: a string of large beads. Originally meant for counting one's adulatory words uttered in the name of the Almighty, these beads on a string had now acquired a very fashionable new function as "worry beads." It seemed to me that idle male grownups were constantly playing with a set of green or amber beads strung on an elastic loop, and they stopped only when they needed both hands to deal with an emergency.

I remember the ornate little utility knives, forks, and spoons that Mashammad brought from Zanjan to sell in Tabriz and Salmas. His double-purpose trips, which had started long before my time, would continue for a while longer. But he said the business wasn't as profitable as it used to be. "Too many competitors," he complained. "He is too old for this now," opined Brother Bagher when Mashammad wasn't around, "He doesn't know exactly what to buy and sell, when and where. And he gets cheated easily." My brother spoke with the obvious confidence of the new generation of business-minded travelers. (Wasn't his recent carpet deal an example of a transaction at the right time and right place?) The new travelers had advantages over Mashammad. For one thing, they could read and write. They could glean market information from newspapers. They knew how the ongoing world war was affecting prices. Some of them were learning dirty tricks from the big operators in the bazaar, tricks like grain hoarding. Some were even dabbling in opium trafficking—an activity forbidden by the law of the land but not by the explicit dicta of the Faith. They also tended to be very competitive. Not Mashammad, the law-abiding, God-fearing, simple, serene, lovable Mashammad! When he said his compulsory daily prayers in Arabic, it was clear even to the ten-year-old me that he mispronounced nearly every word. Father, who had patiently and painstakingly taught me how to say each part of those prayers properly, told me in confidence that Mashammad would be excused by the Almighty. Because *He* knew that this illiterate servant of His didn't know any better; it was the intention that counted, as far as the Almighty was concerned. "Mashammad was no different from a little child," said Father, "and the Almighty understands." I sort of agreed with the Almighty. Mashammad played tic-tac-toe with me and my neighbor kids, and showed us simple magic tricks. He even played cards with the young grownups. But not when Father was around. No grownup was willing to risk looking frivolous to Father.

In just a few years' time Mashammad would supply an irrefutable proof for his deteriorating entrepreneurial abilities as pronounced by Brother Bagher: After making a disastrous business decision that would put an end to his annual trips, the poor man would arrive at my house one early evening with a very large bundle. It contained 200 horse whips, he said, which he had purchased in Zanjan on his way back from the holy shrine in Mashad. The kind of whips used exclusively by the operators of *doroshkehs*—the traditional horse-drawn cabs—to improve their horses' mileage. "I purchased them wholesale at an absolutely rock-bottom price," he would happily announce, planning to sell them in Tabriz and Salmas. Mashammad's hopes for a hefty profit, however, would be dashed by an embittered old doroshkeh driver's cruel reaction to his first attempt at sales: "Have you lost your mind? Haven't you seen all the new motorized cabs running around in Tabriz these days, fast putting us all out of work? No sane doroshkeh-driver in this city will feel like investing in a new whip. Maybe you can sell a couple in your little village Salmas, where motorized taxis are not yet in operation."

But this was still in the future. In the meantime, Mashammad was impressed by what and how much the young amateurs like my brother were capable of. He took special pride in Bagher's inter-city transactions, which he was certain were inspired by his own example. Not long after my brother's bicycle was brought home, Mashammad visited us on one of his periodical journeys. The sight of the wind horse parked in our courtyard, waiting to be sold on Bagher's next trip in the fall or winter, reminded him of his own younger days, when he had delivered milk on a donkey. He wondered if he could now start selling wind horses to his village delivery boys, but he dismissed the idea when he learned how expensive the fancy machines were. He shared my sense of amazement at how the headlight of the wind horse worked and illuminated the entire courtyard—with no plug-in facility in my electricity-free house—by merely twirling the pedal. When my brother gave me a joyride on the wind horse around our courtyard, Mashammad was tempted to try it too, he said, "but only when your father isn't home."

I was pleasantly surprised and amused by what Lady Saria the Pious called Mashammad's lack of a "sense of dignity befitting his age." After all, he looked just a few years younger than my septuagenarian father at the time, but I am sure now that he was at least twenty years younger. "I have seen people riding wind horses on the pavement in Tehran," he said with a sigh, "the ride looked so nice and smooth, I wish I were young again and able to learn how to ride a wind horse." He and Bagher agreed that there was really only one road in Tabriz where the ride could be enjoyed: "the Paved Avenue"—so named informally and informatively, because it was the only paved road in the city at the time. Its official name, "Pahlavi Avenue" after the Shah's father, was only recognizable by the literate minority of citizens. Mashammad, as well as my brother, knew that we couldn't attempt the experiment on the Paved Avenue, which would be regarded by Father as a highly improper show of whimsy. (A distant cousin of mine whose rich family exchanged visits with mine only during the annual *Nowruz* celebrations, had recently taken part in a biking competition organized for the city youth. His father paid for this lapse in proper upbringing of his offspring by losing all respect in my father's eyes: "Was it necessary for the young man to show off in the streets?" Father asked me and my brother, answering himself with another question: "Why couldn't he take his pleasure rides in the privacy of his father's huge courtyard?" Father wouldn't hear of any value attributed to races, or to organized sports in general, for that matter. They were "nothing but a cleverly disguised effort by the Government to prepare the nation's youth for military service.")

THE BIKE SAT IN THE CORNER of the courtyard for months before Bagher's departure for Tehran. On an autumn day, Mother kissed my brother good-by at the door—the bus terminal being no place for a respectable woman to be seen at, unless she herself had to travel. Then Bagher, Father, I, and the bicycle walked to the bus station. The bicycle was loaded on top of the bus together with all the passengers' numerous pieces of luggage. It would accompany my brother all the way to Tehran, unless it was sold somewhere along the way. It was a difficult piece of luggage to load. The porter had to put large pieces of cardboard around its sharp and uneven parts, so it wouldn't damage the other pieces of traditional luggage, which mainly consisted of large parcels wrapped in soft cotton, kept together with safety pins. I considered the extra fees that Bagher would have to pay for handling this awkward article each time it was unloaded for presentation to a potential customer. How could he possibly make a profit? Was the bicycle really intended to make money? A mystery, indeed.

"Are you going to ride it on the pavement in Tehran?" I finally decided to ask my brother in my softest and most tentative voice, when father had walked away momentarily to chat with a friend. "No," he replied emphatically, "I'll probably sell it before we reach Tehran." But I sensed that he was being careful now that Father was walking back toward us. I wished I could go to Tehran with him and experience that ride at "wind speed" on a paved surface, away from Father's sphere of influence.

(My wish would come true a few years later: More streets would be paved in Tabriz, and I would have a new school friend, Habib, who'd let me use his bicycle to learn how to ride on the paved streets around his own house. Safely far away from my house and from Father's work place in the bazaar, I would treasure my occasional short after-school hours spent biking with Habib. A bad fall and an injured knee would, alas, put an end to the frivolity. It would happen on the freshly paved wide avenue that now connected the city center to the Army headquarters, and tempted every young man in possession of a bicycle. Noticing how scared I was after the fall, lest my secret should be revealed to Father, Habib's resourceful uncle would take me to the local butcher shop, buy a piece of fresh red meat, place it on my knee, and wrap a cotton rag tightly around it. This ancient remedy would, miraculously, eliminate my limp and most of my pain. I would keep the bandage in place and hidden from my parents until the next morning. Then the stale meat would start to smell. I would have to confess to Mother and ask her to think of something to avert the potential disaster of being found out by Father. Mother, always as mindful of Father's impossible rules as I was, would save me, but only after extracting a firm promise from me not to engage in this dangerous activity again until I finished high school. Then, using yet another folk recipe, she would replace the meat bandage with a small disk of freshly concocted, odorless patty of salted flour dough.)

My brother's trip to Tehran was apparently uneventful. I wasn't surprised by the report that the bike had accompanied him all the way to Tehran on account of no serious offers made in Mianeh, Zanjan, or Qazvin, his three longish stops. Now it had to wait for an acceptable offer in Tehran.

The long summer ended. I started sixth grade and almost forgot about the wind horse that had stood so invitingly for so long in the corner of my courtyard.

ANSWERING THE KNOCK ON THE DOOR one afternoon in late autumn, I found an exhausted Mashammad, covered by road dust, squatted on top of his soft luggage. He had arrived, not too unexpectedly, from his latest pilgrimage to Mashad. "Tell your mother to add water to the *abgusht* for dinner tonight," he said with his usual big smile, "you have an extra mouth to feed." Then he waited at the door until I informed Mother of his arrival. When she had properly covered her body and hair on account of male presence, Mashammad entered the courtyard and greeted Mother before she had a chance to say hello first. (Not quite right, I said to myself. He obviously hadn't learned the strong recommendation by the scholars of the Faith that a man should never greet a woman first. But he would be excused, I remembered my father saying, because he didn't know any better, he was like an innocent child.) "May your pilgrimage be accepted by the Almighty," said Mother. "May you also have the privilege to take the trip," replied Mashammad, before I directed him to the guest room and Mother started to brew some tea for him.

Mashammad washed up, said his totally mispronounced afternoon prayers, and sat down to rest and sip his tea. Mother went to the kitchen to add the proverbial water to the soup. We still had an hour or so before Father would come home from work. Mashammad was already relaxed and in his customary jovial mood. He took a small, full bag out of his large parcel and placed it on the mantel; it obviously contained his Mashad souvenirs for the family. I knew that it would be impolite to open the bag and claim my share; I had to contain my curiosity at any cost for hours. He asked me about my schooling. "Whatever you do," he said "don't quit school." He was very appreciative of the fact that, on a previous trip, I had taught him how to write his own name. "You know," he announced proudly, "this time going to Mashad, I actually signed my own name on the travel permit, instead of giving the police a fingerprint." I, too, felt proud for my contribution toward his minimal literacy. "But I wish I had learned to read signs," he sighed, "I almost got arrested in Tehran for not being able to read, you know." Surprised, I asked for details. Surely, being illiterate was not an offense; otherwise a large majority of the country's population would be in prison. Mashammad looked anxious. Perhaps he'd said too much. Yet it was not like him to refuse an explanation. "Can you keep a secret from your father?" he asked. Yes, of course I could. "Okay, it happened last week in Tehran," he was now relieved to report, "while I was staying with your old brother Kazem's in-laws." This was clearly going to be a long story, but we were both ready for it. My mother called me from the kitchen and handed me another cup of tea for him.

"And who happens to drop in that day?" Mashammad asked and went on. "Your brother Bagher, of course. And, yes, he comes on his wind horse. He offers me a ride! You'll keep your promise, right? Your father should never find out, okay? Okay. It turns out that Bagher hasn't been able to sell the wind horse yet. He takes me for a ride on the pavement—in Tehran every street seems to be paved, did you know? Isn't it amazing? Anyway, he is riding his wind horse and I am sitting on his luggage rack, which I have cushioned with my jacket. You should have been there and seen us! The ride is so smooth, and the cool wind feels so nice on my face. I tell him how I wished to ride the yel-aati by myself. He understands. He smiles and he takes me to a quieter street, paved of course. Then he teaches me how to peddle. And then he lets me do it all by myself on a slightly downhill section of the street. He says it is easier to learn there. Be very cautious, he warns me. I *am* very cautious, of course, but before I know it, the slope gets much sharper. I have lost sight of Bagher. Soon I lose control and hit a bypassing donkey. I pray to God for protection, and I promise God that I'll feed seven poor people next Friday eve. Sure enough, praise be to God, the donkey, the wind horse, and I all escape injury. Not even a nose bleed. Not even a scratch on the donkey or on the wind horse. But then this cop suddenly appears, I don't know from where. I am so scared. The cop is, you know, one of those young, educated sort who obviously thinks everybody was born knowing how to read and write, especially if they live in the capital city. I know, I know; everybody should go to school; have it from me, Heydar, don't ever quit school; it is a different world out there now, very different from what it was when I was your age… . Anyway, the cop comes to me and starts to shout. 'Uncle, are you blind? Can't you see the big sign that says no bicycles are allowed on this part of the road?' He admonishes me as if I were a kid. I am filled with fear and embarrassment. What would my relatives think if I am arrested? How would Bagher explain all this childish behavior to your father? I plead to God once more …, more urgently this time. I beg Him again to save me for the sake of my beloved Master whose holy tomb in Mashad I have just touched and kissed. You don't know how scared I am. I am trembling and calling my Master's name over and over again, and asking *him* to beg God on my behalf....

"And then the miracle happens: the cop takes a good look at me, and I don't know what he sees on my face or above my head. Perhaps a band of light, a halo, lent me by my Master resting in Mashad, may I be sacrificed at his blessed feet... . All of a sudden the cop softens, God be praised. 'Uncle,' he addresses me with respect, 'I see that you have made a mistake,' he says, 'and I trust you will never do it again. Good-bye!'"

Russian Movies at Your Own Risk

"In the eyes of the Almighty," I hear the preacher saying, "we are all equal, all of us, from the poorest peasant to the richest man in the world; until our thoughts and actions place us squarely on the road to Heaven or Hell, as the case may be." Aware that his audience includes a fair number of academics, he goes on: "Whether it be a teacher of physical sciences,"—here, in recognition of the university crowd, he makes a sweeping motion with his left hand over the rows of us professors in attendance—"or whether it be a learned man,"—now he turns his right hand toward his own chest for illustration—"we are all equally responsible for our deeds. And every little deed counts. Every little deed. Let us all be warned."

The theme of the sermon, "every little deed counts," is relevant to the occasion: we are attending a memorial service for a colleague's mother, a woman who appears to have performed a great number of good little deeds during her long life. This is an all-male service—an all-female version is in progress simultaneously, elsewhere of course. I have never met or seen this preacher before. He seems a little too young for the job, too well-dressed for a man of God, and too self-assured for his age. Why hasn't our bereaved colleague asked an older, wiser, and more respectable man of cloth to preside over the ceremonies? Surely there are quite a few of them in this city of Shiraz, "The Citadel of

Knowledge," as it has been known for centuries. Maybe this man was preferred by the grieving family because he was thought to be more appealing to the "modern" academics. Or, maybe the surroundings, the very university hall in which we are gathered, the Shah's picture on the wall, and the furnishings, weren't acceptable to a genuine man of God. The surroundings are certainly far from traditional. Until just a few decades ago, memorial services were all held in mosques or pious homes; certainly never in a secular school hall. The congregation always sat on the carpeted floor, and the preacher on the pulpit or another elevated device. This time-honored option is surely still available to mourners in every city in Iran. It is, in fact, still the prevailing norm now, in the late 1960s. Perhaps our colleague chose the present venue because he knew that most of the invited participants, all in modern suits, were very conscious of the crease in their well-pressed trousers and would think twice before sitting on any floor, except at home where most of them changed to pajamas upon arrival.

"I know this guy," whispers the man sitting next to me, a colleague from the Department of Biology. He is referring to the preacher, of course, who is now expanding on his chosen topic, giving authoritative examples of surprisingly large reactions to various small actions. My companion doesn't hide his disdain for the preacher. "I wouldn't have come if it weren't absolutely necessary," he says. Noticing that I know nothing about the man, he smiles, shows surprise, and stops whispering. We both settle in our seats for a lecture that promises to be even longer than the customary forty-five minutes for such occasions.

The long, familiar verses from old sages, which the preacher recites to corroborate his points, have a sort of hypnotizing effect on me. I am losing him and starting to daydream. I revisit similar seances from long ago: dozens of sermons on monumental consequences of small acts. I remember how, as a child, I was instructed by my elders to take every single one of my acts, good or evil, very seriously. Memories of my evil acts have managed somehow to survive more vividly. They are overwhelming; they can certainly spoil a daydream. Take the candy-fish incident, for example.

I AM PROBABLY SIX YEARS OLD. I am holding my mother's hand in a crowded old bazaar in my home city of Tabriz. We are standing at the counter of a candy store. Mother is waiting in line, intending to buy a "sugar cone" for a wedding gift. These extra-large, solid cones, to be chipped into small lumps at home and used as sweeteners for tea, are standard utilitarian gifts among ordinary citizens of Tabriz for any joyous occasion. There seem to be hundreds of cones on the shelves of this store, all factory-wrapped in the customary blue paper. But I am more interested in the huge eye-level counter covered with trays of delicious-looking rock candy. I ask Mother if I could have one of those red-and-green candies shaped like roosters. She says no, because we are going to a wedding party in a few hours, where we'll have treats of all kinds; and so much sugar is not good for me anyway; and what would Father say if I developed zits on my face as a result of eating too much sugar? But I couldn't wait, I decide privately. The large pieces, in various shapes, from cats and rabbits to chickens and roosters, are far away, but I can easily reach a tempting tiny fish. And I grab it when nobody is looking. I know I shouldn't do this, but I do it anyway. I regret it right away, as soon as I manage to hide the fish in my mouth and start to suck on it discreetly. But I will regret it much more in the near future.

Now it is a few weeks after the wedding. Mother and I are attending a *marsia* session for women, organized and hosted by a devout household in our neighborhood. We are sitting on a thick carpet in a large room packed with women and children. An old *marsia-khan*, the only male presence in the room, is presiding from a wooden armchair. He is going through the perfunctory, brief sermon before he starts his songs of lamentation for the Martyrs of the Faith—the real purpose of all marsia gatherings. I am eyeing the mouth-watering dates and cookies on a plate in front of me, which I am forbidden to touch until the sermon and the ensuing sad songs come to an end. The white-haired preacher, with his long and hennaed beard, looks and sounds very different from the much younger live one currently lecturing us in this hall. The old man's examples of tiny actions causing colossal reactions are similar to the ones I am vaguely hearing right now, but his tone has an unimpeachable authority. I can hear him clearly after all these years. "Woe to the servant of God who earns himself the eternal fires of Hell in the Hereafter by stealing," he exclaims. "Yes, stealing even a tiny coin, a loaf of bread, or a lump of sugar." This is enough to fill any self-respecting kid like me with fear. Did he have to mention the lump of sugar too? "In the case of the loaf of bread," he qualifies his assertion, "the sinner would be forgiven, of course, if—let me emphasize, *if*—he was desperately hungry." A glimpse of hope for me, perhaps? What about desperately needing a lump of sugar or a rock candy? But no further exemptions are forthcoming; the preacher pauses for a few seconds and switches to the much-anticipated lamentations. Woe to me then? Is there a way out of Hell for me, this little obedient servant of God? Would I perhaps be forgiven by the Almighty if I resist the temptation to touch those dates now, even when the old man leaves and the audience takes a tea break from the collective weeping and wailing?

THE RAISED VOICE OF THE PRESIDING PREACHER perks me up. He is now mentioning physics and biology in connection with small acts and big consequences. But I, in my half-asleep state, seem to have missed the beginning of this section of the lecture, so I have no trouble going back to my reminiscences.

Now it is the summer after my second year in elementary school and I am sitting in the corner of one of the several unfurnished rooms in my large old house. With me is Mamadali, my best friend and next-door neighbor. We are admiring his three lovely little kittens he has brought over for a visit. He has just released the very young creatures from their protective basket. The kittens start running around in every direction. I notice that I have left the door ajar and one of the kittens is about to venture out. I decide to protect it from potential danger. I get up and, running fast to shut the door, I step on another kitten. It dies instantly. Mamadali and I start to cry uncontrollably, and he attacks me with clenched fists. He can't hurt me much—he is almost two years younger. What he is doing to me is nothing anyway, I am certain, compared to the punishment God has in store for murderers like me. How much of my crying is from the sorrow of loss, and how much from the fear of retribution by the Almighty? How am I to know? Mother hears us from the kitchen and runs to the scene of the crime. She tries to console us. It wasn't really my fault, she tells me, and God would never punish a person, let alone a kid, for an obviously honest mistake, an accident. She gives us snacks of raisins and roasted wheat and reminds us of the time, not too long ago, when Mamadali and I took loving care of a wounded, hungry, and thirsty little sparrow for several days until it could fly again and perch on top of our old mulberry tree. "Think of how much God will reward you for that good deed," she reassures us. Then she sends Mamadali home with the basket containing the surviving kittens. While we are burying the evidence next to the root of the small plum tree in our courtyard, I am still filled with that strange mixture of sorrow and fear. It takes Mother the rest of the day to convince me that I haven't done anything deserving punishment in the afterworld. Mamadali takes no more than an hour to come back to my house, all forgiveness. He is also reassured by his grandmother that no intentional sin has been committed, and we are both safe.

I AM FAINTLY AWARE THAT I am still at this memorial service and that the preacher has now switched to philosophy and psychology. My comrade-in-mourning awakens me with a soft laughter blown into my ear. "Wake up! This part you just have to hear," he says. I listen for a minute and discover the reason for his amusement. The preacher is talking about "*Farvid*, the great *Frangi* specialist," as he puts it. This mispronunciation of Sigmund Freud's name is not at all surprising—the preacher has no doubt encountered the Western name only in Persian transliteration. Perhaps in this case the misreading was partially caused by the fact that "Farvid" rhymes with the Persian name "*Fardid*." Ahmad Fardid, whose name is also dropped more than once by the preacher for the benefit of what he considers a literate audience, is a controversial, contemporary Iranian philosopher. According to his devout followers, Fardid "has resolved certain difficulties that Heidegger encountered in his philosophical scheme, which he could not tackle himself." We don't know it yet, but three decades hence, Fardid will be considered to be one of the early ideologues of the 1979 Revolution in Iran.

This memorial lecture is clearly going to be a long one, I decide, and I have lost its thread. If I had listened carefully, maybe I would have found out what Sigmund Farvid and Ahmad Fardid had to do with small actions causing huge reactions. Or with each other, for that matter, except for their rhyming last names. But it is too late now, I decide. Back to my own memories.

Now I am a few years older. Having been reminded repeatedly of momentous consequences of our tiniest acts, and aware of my own imperfect record, which included the candy theft and the kitten murder, I have decided on a course of atonement. It is the holy month of Ramazan, the fasting month. I can't wait until I am of the responsible age, when fasting and praying will be mandatory for me. So, determined on a long-term rehearsal, I have joined Father and Mother in fasting every day of the lunar month—the whole long day, like dutiful adults; not just half the day, like some gluttonous kids. I am hoping to turn myself eventually to an exemplary servant of the Lord. I have just learned from a cleric on the pulpit that the rewards for fasting would be more than doubled and many sins forgiven, if I do something extra. Thus I have decided to supplement my fasting by following the cleric's explicit directions: After breaking my fast on a specified evening of the Holy Month, I have stayed awake and repeatedly performed the prescribed lengthy prayer. One hundred times, exactly as the man of God recommended. I have perhaps spent two hours on the task and proudly completed the sequence. I am in dire need of sleep, but I am happily basking in a feeling of great accomplishment to be envied, I am sure, even by the most pious, grown-up servants of the Almighty.

Perhaps triggered by a half-heard word from the ongoing sermon that I have stopped following, the daydreams have been fast-forwarded: I am now about twelve. I am intently listening to a sermon by my favorite clergyman Sheikh Hussen. (A friend and I, both in sixth grade, both looking forward anxiously to starting high school soon, have recently discovered this particular man of God. We took an immediate liking to Sheikh Hussen as soon as he announced his opposition to the opinion, expressed by some of his colleagues, that what is taught in the public high schools is detrimental to our faith.) Today, Sheikh Hussen has explained the difference between the two kinds of duties we have as observant believers. "Duty to God and duty to His servants," he has said, and he goes on to elaborate: "We pray, we fast, and we take pilgrimage to holy shrines, for instance. This is all to fulfill our duties to God. On the other hand, we respect His servants' rights to their personal safety, their privacy, and their property as part of our duties to *them*." Sheikh Hussen is now adding something that leaves a deep impression on me. "If you neglect your duties of the first kind," he explains," say, you miss an obligatory prayer or, God forbid, take an alcoholic drink under Satan's influence, then you have committed a sin of the first kind, and God will forgive you after a sincere act of repentance on your part." So far so good, I say to myself. "But earning His forgiveness for the second kind of sin is not that simple," he goes on. "If you cause anyone bodily harm or steal anything from anyone, or hurt anyone's feelings, you must first secure the forgiveness of the party involved." *This* is a revelation to me.

"Is it true, what Sheikh Hussen says about the two kinds of duties?" I ask my father as soon as he comes home from work that evening. Father confirms it. It makes sense, I decide. In a future decade, I'll learn a new name for these sins of the first kind: "victimless crimes." For now, I have to deal with those of the second kind. This is definitely worrisome: I am reminded, of course, of the candy-fish episode. Evidently, that atonement session that I so enthusiastically went through a few years back, was in no way sufficient for absolution. I must talk to that candy-shop owner and ask for his forgiveness, shouldn't I? Yes, no ifs or buts about it. The shop is still there. In fact my friends and I go there often to spend a great part of our allowances. Confessing to my theft is of course embarrassing, so I devise an indirect approach. I go to the shop one day after school, buy a small chocolate bar and casually broach the subject. "A friend of mine, who used to live around here, very close to your store," I begin, "tells me that when he was a little kid and knew no better, he once lifted a candy fish … ." To my delight, the shop owner interrupts me with a big smile and says, "Don't worry. Your friend sounds like he has grown into a good kid. Tell him that it is all forgiven and forgotten." What a relief!

My reverie is rudely interrupted again, this time by a very urgent poke in the rib, from my neighbor. "I can't let you miss this," he alerts me. "Honestly! The guy just promised to treat us to a personal experience about truly big consequences of very tiny acts." I open my eyes wide, shake the daydreams out of my head, and hear an extraordinary story that makes me regret having missed so much of this long sermon.

"This is about one of my very own acquaintances," the flamboyant preacher says and starts to relate the story with great relish. "It is about a prominent man of commerce, whom most of you know. But he will remain nameless today. He told me about his first-hand experience recently, and I have absolutely no hesitation in believing him, for he is a godly man—in spite of his Frangi suit and necktie." Obviously pleased with this demonstration of his open mind toward Western attire, and having given this subtle message of hope to his fully necktie-adorned audience, the speaker goes on: "He told me that his wife is, like him, of a dark complexion with black hair and brown eyes. So are their first two children, he said. Thus you can imagine how shocked the parents were when God blessed them with a truly blond, green-eyed baby boy. They couldn't believe their eyes. There was nobody in their extended families whose physical features could justify this turn of events. They knew of no Frangi ancestry. Yes, there were a few men among their acquaintances who had married German or Russian women; there were also some Americans and some Englishmen in town, who worked at the University or other Government institutions. But this couple's socialization with foreigners was very limited. You can no doubt guess the ensuing unhappy state of affairs... ."

Encouraged by the peaked interest of the audience in this potentially juicy story, the preacher is getting louder and more excited by the second. "Yes, suspicion started to poison the life of the good family. Everyone, including all the neighbors, got suspicious of everyone else. The man got suspicious of the wife; the wife got suspicious of the husband... ." Here I use the opportunity to return my neighbor's poke in the rib and ask him in a soft voice if he shares my bemusement, my inability to understand the reason for the *wife's* reported suspicion about her husband. The preacher is obviously enjoying the suspense he has created: "The couple was on the verge of divorce. Advised and urged by friends and family, they consulted many doctors and psychologists in Shiraz, but to no avail... . Until they were finally directed to a prominent doctor in Tehran." Here comes another reference to Sigmund Farvid, I predict to myself, but no more names are dropped. From what I hear next, the doctor in Tehran must belong to a higher caste of specialists:

"They were fortunate to take the advice," the preacher now informs us. "They traveled to Tehran, without much hope, and had a consultation with the specialist. The diagnosis took a long time and cost a great deal of money. The doctor asked them many questions, some very personal and difficult as you would expect, before he was at last able to pinpoint the cause of this aberration in nature: It turned out that on the very night the baby was conceived, the couple had watched a Russian movie."

The Guardian of Rhythm and Rhyme

"I have composed almost eleven kilos of poetry," announced Mr. Parnian. He was repeating the unusual claim he had made the day before. Now he gently put down a sizable bundle of paper on the spare desk in my office at Pahlavi University. Then he smiled shyly and said, "And, for your perusal, here are some samples I promised you yesterday."

I didn't remember his full name. Maybe I never knew it. We hadn't seen each other for some 16 years. The day before his sudden appearance in my office, I had run into him in a teahouse. He was working, he said, as an assistant to a pharmacist who knew my brother in Tabriz, my hometown. He'd learned through his boss that I was now living and teaching in his hometown of Shiraz. I recognized his melancholic face and sleepy eyes right away. And I remembered his pen-name, "Parnian"—the Persian word for a variety of silk. He had used the name for signing his poetry when he was a college student in Tabriz. I had just started high school then and, like everyone else in the neighborhood, I knew him as the timid, disheveled young man from Shiraz. He lodged in a house not too far from our Ali Khan Close. He often visited a college friend living a few doors from my house, also from his hometown. We, the junior high school students, were impressed by these two young men and by their recitations of the sonnets written by the great Persian poets of Shiraz seven centuries earlier. Mr. Parnian always accomplished this without notes and at the slightest indication of interest on the part of a prospective audience. I was especially in awe of his memory, because of my own inability in memorizing more than a few lines of verse out of many assigned to us in school. Having captured the attention of an audience, Mr. Parnian would throw in a sonnet of his own, the last line of which would, like those of the sonnets from the beloved Hafez of Shiraz, identify the author by name or pseudonym, "Parnian" in his case. I think we, the kids, were the ones who started calling him "Mr. Parnian" and the name stuck.

After delivering this large parcel of samples of his poetry to my office, Mr. Parnian didn't stay for the customary cup of tea. He was in a hurry to get back to work, the source of his daily bread, as he put it. I looked over some of his verses as soon as I had a chance that afternoon. Most of the poems were like the ones I remembered from his college days in Tabriz, but now quite a few of them registered serious grievances. Not just the expected, old-fashioned lamentations over lost love and lost youth. But also bitter, defiant complaints about contemporary poets who didn't begin to understand, much less appreciate, his millennium-old classical style. I was used to similar grumblings from my eldest brother Kazem and his colleagues, all poets of classical persuasion, who enjoyed making fun of the "illiterate pretenders, so-called modern Persian poets, who dared to call their formless and rhythmless utterances poetry." My chance encounter with Mr. Parnian in Shiraz had just brought to light my old memories of him and his encounters with my brother Bagher, who was a dozen years older than me but a dozen years younger than our brother

Kazem, the poet. Bagher never wrote any poetry himself, but had studied literature, and considered himself an expert of sorts on the subject. He detested the new "alternative" poetry as much as Kazem and Mr. Parnian did. And he had very high standards when it came to "real" poetry. "Every poet deserving the title has one good piece," he had said more than once, "maybe two or, very rarely, three." He never forgot to add, "Yes, I am including our dear brother Kazem, of course." He had even memorized many of these often-unique samples from various poets who passed his strict qualifying tests.

The one composition of Mr. Parnian which Brother Bagher found acceptable, just barely, was about a supposed dream of a "stray" fledgling: The young dreamer in the piece is an admirer and follower of Nima Yooshij, "the father of modern poetry in Iran." In the dream, old masters of classical Persian poetry take leave of their centuries-old tombs and appear collectively to admonish the young man. And they attack Nima and his modernist comrades, as vehemently as strictures of rhythm and rhyme allow. "Challenge this pretender, your guru, to write just a single sonnet, if he can, in our time-honored style," the great Hafez proposes in the dream, "and if he succeeds, we promise to sit down and listen to his modern songs." What impressed Bagher was not the story, which was quite unoriginal, of course, but the way it was put together—the customary, clever play on words: An insult here, targeting the rebel poets, which sounded like praise on first hearing; an allusion there, to mythical events and characters, which was open to two or, preferably, more different interpretations. Unless you were well versed in the art, you'd miss it all, almost. My literature teacher, also a devotee of the old school, tried hard to educate me and my classmates on these subtleties. But my own attempts at classical verse produced less than presentable results.

THE SIXTEEN-YEAR-OLD IMAGES of impromptu meetings of neighbors and friends in Ali Khan Close on those summer weekend afternoons in Tabriz were still vivid in my memory—they still are as I write this after almost seventy years. These informal gatherings took place in the wider part of our cul de sac, near its entrance, "the Mouth" as everybody called it. Large wooden gates had once stood here to protect the inhabitants from burglars—times had been harder for the general public at the time, but evidently not for the then prosperous residents of Ali Khan Close. (Mr. Parnian's cul de sac, near ours, was another formerly rich "gated community" with its huge and sturdy old doors at its entrance still intact but now permanently open. Had its residents been richer at the time, I wondered, or just more cautious than those of Ali Khan Close?)

You could casually start one of these informal weekend gatherings or join an ongoing one; you could leave it anytime at will, or take a break and come back to it later. Assuming, of course, that you were a male of any age, or a female under seven. Womenfolk never congregated in this most public part of Ali Khan Close, nearer the Mouth. Only the older women of the cul de sac would sometimes stop and chat with the men, for just a minute or two. From the Mouth you could see the main road traffic: it consisted of loaded donkeys, horse-drawn *arabas* and *droskhies*, and an occasional motorized vehicle. The typical air-polluting emissions were still purely organic and largely contributed by the working animals. A few very old men like my father considered it below their dignity to stand in the middle of a residential street, or at its mouth, for prolonged conversations. When one of these senior citizens of Ali Khan Close passed by, the group showed its collective respect with lowered voices, bowed heads, and polite greetings. The male chattering never took place in the other parts of Ali Khan Close. The middle part, still quite wide, was usually occupied by the neighborhood kids at play. The very end, the narrowest and most secure part, which terminated at the gate to my house, was reserved for women's brief gatherings. For a true get-together, the women preferred enclosed courtyards of individual houses. The men highly approved of this preference.

Whatever the weekend topic of discussion at the Mouth happened to be, those men who could read and write, peppered their conversation with quotations in verse, both in Persian and in Azeri Turkish. Some were obviously very competent at this and had an appropriate quote for every occasion. Some just listened. As it had always been the case in Iran, gross exaggeration was not just permitted in applying the quotes to the situation at hand; it was actually required for emphasis, and it was enthusiastically applauded. There was this richer neighbor, for instance, who owned a radio set and enjoyed dispensing free wisdom on world politics. The man was exceedingly fond of the late President Franklin Roosevelt of the United States, but, for some reason, not very approving of the incumbent president at the time, Harry Truman. He once indicated his sorrow at the passing away of the former, and his displeasure with the latter's presidency, by declaiming the familiar couplet: "It's only after the brilliant Sun leaves the stage/That the awful bat finds a chance to dance." Most outrageous exaggerations were of course reserved for songs of adulation, in which the physical features of the beloved were worshipfully sketched and the hardships of hopeless love lamented. The audiences always knew, for example, that no beloved with a mouth larger than a pistachio nut, a belly broader than a hair, or lips less red than a rose in full bloom was worthy of a great poet's adulation. Nor was any beloved with hair shorter than a lasso—with which to entrap and steal the hearts of flocks of unsuspecting victims of love—worth singing about.

"Mr. Parnian is not always *there*," my brother Bagher said before one of those Friday afternoon get-togethers. To pinpoint the exact locality where the possible cause of Mr. Parnian's problem resided, Brother Bagher tapped himself on the head with a pointed index finger. He was answering my question on the quality of Mr. Parnian's poetry. "And when he *is* there," he added dismissively, "he can only manage a mediocre imitation of Hafez." But if Hafez was as astonishingly great as we all believe he was, a younger neighbor and I both wanted to know, then wouldn't even a mediocre imitation of his songs be worth something? My brother was adamant. "A poet who doesn't have anything to say himself, and must say what Hafez has already said six hundred years ago, should either say it better than Hafez or shut up," he asserted. He emphasized the finality of his edict by a fast downward motion of his right hand. This was an extreme view to most of the audience. Didn't everybody know that it was simply unthinkable to surpass Hafez? Wasn't the very popular, contemporary poet Shahriar, a famous local son now living away in the capital city, unabashedly proud of following in the glorious footsteps of Hafez, the master?

"Let him be," said Mr. Shabestari, the retired school teacher who came out of his house, cup in hand, sipping his habitual tea which, according to my brother, was often secretly fortified with vodka. He had overheard us and was gently admonishing my brother. "Don't you see that the guy is in love?" The old teacher always listened to Mr. Parnian's recitations with fascination and admiration. He bobbed his head sympathetically when the poet sang of his deep "sorrow of separation from the beloved." Mr. Shabestari praised the poet's artistry, which he said even held the promise of one day *approaching* that of Hafez. "What separation? What beloved?" asked my brother rhetorically, having made sure that the poet wasn't within earshot by chance. "There has to be some togetherness with a beloved before you can start talking of separation, for God's sake! This guy is in love with an imaginary beloved." This didn't seem to bother Mr. Shabestari at all; he didn't see any necessity for the physical existence of an actual beloved. What was the matter with Brother Bagher anyway? Didn't he see the beauty in the poet's lamentations? Who cared now about the hypothetical beloved to whom the great Hafez himself had devoted his magnificent sonnets? "Besides," the old teacher addressed my brother exclusively, obviously assuming that only he among us would appreciate the heft of the argument, "you should know better than I that love and separation is not necessarily, nor often, of the earthly variety. The reader or listener chooses his own interpretation. The beloved could be, as it often is in mystic verses, the Almighty Himself. And separation may mean a deep feeling of temporary failure in being completely absorbed in His Glory." Some of us kids remembered at this point that we had a soccer game to start.

BUT THERE WAS GOSSIP IN THE AIR about Ali Khan Close, which had the potential of proving my brother wrong. Several residents had been informed by the itinerant washwoman about sightings in a distant neighborhood, of Mr. Parnian riding a "wind horse"—a bicycle. "I saw him near the front door of Rubab the singer's house," the woman confided to my neighbor Saria—"Lady Saria the Pious" to most people in the neighborhood. "What business he had there," the report continued, "a single young man, on a wind horse near that house, is none of my business, of course, but you know what kind of reputation Rubab has." Saria did not approve of sinful gossiping, but agreed that the young man's renting a wind horse to chase a young female singer in that questionable district of the city was more sinful than the washwoman's gossiping. "Wind horses are responsible for a great deal of sinful activity these days," Lady Saria opined, reminding the neighbors of a recent incident in our own small community: a few weeks earlier, a young thief was able to get away easily on his bike, having lifted a samovar from my own house in bright daylight, and nobody had been able to catch him. Without a bike, such a crime would have been absolutely impossible in Ali Khan Close, said Saria. The washwoman and my mother both had to agree.

The reputation that was being discussed was that of a *sazanda*—this term applied to a typical member of any group of professional female musicians, hired for festive occasions, mainly wedding parties for women. Some said that sazandas were also hired to perform in mixed company, but almost nobody in Ali Khan Close seemed to believe this about Rubab. It was now too late for me, having just reached the responsible male age of fourteen, to attend those women's parties, but I had happy memories of accompanying my mother to many such gatherings while I still passed as an "innocent boy." I had watched the very popular and pretty Rubab the sazanda sing and play her *tar*. I had also seen her once rehearsing with her colleagues. This was when my mother and a friend of hers took me along to visit Rubab in her home, where she lived with her sazanda mother. We were there to book her group's services for the upcoming wedding of the friend's son.

(My mother never tired of telling the story of the single occasion in her married life on which she had won an argument with my father: it had happened five years before I was born. My only sister was getting married; my father's religious stand against music making was firm and clear. There had always been music in the household, of course, but all easily hidden from Father. Hiring professional musicians for a wedding, however, could not be managed underground; so Mother threatened not to have anything to do with the wedding until Father consented to the hiring. Everyone in the bride's and groom's families was pleasantly surprised that the bluff had worked, but they knew somehow that it would probably never work again. Sazandas were thus commissioned for the wedding party to be attended by women and children only, as Mother gleefully reported to me after all those years. Father, as expected, had stayed away from his own house for the duration.)

What the washwoman and Lady Saria the Pious disapproved about Rubab seemed to consist of several infractions: living in a household without male supervision, not covering her face in public as diligently as expected of a godly young woman, talking to strange men, and—assuming, God forbid, that there was any truth to the rumors—letting men hear her singing voice. This attitude on the part of Lady Saria was considered extreme by my mother and her circle of female friends, although they all professed to be religious and would never sing themselves, or play an instrument, in the presence of men. When they heard of appearances of Mr. Parnian and his rented wind horse in the vicinity of Rubab's home, they expressed understanding for Mr. Parnian's predicament. "What would you do," one woman put sympathetically, "if you were a lonely young man living away from home, wanting to ask for a girl's hand, but had no relatives who could talk to the girl's parents on your behalf?" "Yes," countered another female resident of Ali Khan Close, "but couldn't he send a neighbor, say one of us, as a surrogate parent?"

So, perhaps the object of Mr. Parian's love was real after all, I thought. I put myself in the young poet's shoes. I was certain that I would also fall in love with the beautiful Rubab if I were Mr. Parnian. Who but a singer would be worthy of a poet's love? Wasn't every literate young man in Tabriz, who had read a few French novels in translation, in love with a singer or a dancer? At least with one of the singers Radio Tabriz had made famous—albeit sight unseen?

"There is a chance Mr. Parnian will stop writing his unhappy songs now," said Brother Bagher, having heard of the rumors of love. "If he gets married, that is." "It'll be a loss for Persian poetry," said Mr. Shabestari, partly to tease Bagher. But it seemed that something bad had happened to the poet. Nobody was sure what, where, or how. Had he proposed to Rubab and been rejected? Had he even actually gone all the way to Rubab's house on his wind horse? Had he been beaten up by the local, self-appointed, male protectors of Rubab's honor for daring to approach her in person, instead of sending a respected old female delegate, as required by the time-honored rules of decency? The only evidence of unrequited love anybody could see was that Mr. Parnian was now more reclusive. "He must be in hiding," mused Bagher, "and trying to compose his masterpiece." Even the poet's college friend on our block didn't know what was really going on. Mr. Shabestari alone was now entrusted by the poet with occasional copies of his latest verses, which were "particularly sorrowful and spiritual" according to the old teacher. The citizens of Ali Khan Close and vicinity waited, concerned and clueless. They only hoped the young poet wouldn't do anything crazy.

Soon Mr. Parnian quit school and vacated his rented room. He disappeared. He'd left for his home city, everyone assumed. We were all left in the dark for many months. When Mr. Shabestari finally heard from him, he shared the news with the neighbors: The young poet was indeed in Shiraz, with his folks, and he was employed as a pharmacy clerk. He had also confided in Mr. Shabestari, the teacher told us, that he "would never, ever get married." Everybody was relieved that he hadn't harmed himself, thank God. In time, his adventures were forgotten and his room was rented by another student, a medical student this time, who was too busy to attend the Friday gatherings.

Rubab left her musical profession, "repented," as the washwoman informed us, and married a respectable, devout, wealthy old widower from the Tabriz bazaar. "Not that there hadn't been many other, younger suitors," the woman said, "but they were all of Mr. Parnian's type; all poor and jobless. One of them had even expected Rubab to continue working as a sazanda and—would you believe it?—support him while he looked for a job." Other sazandas had to be found for women's wedding parties, and no male citizen saw Rubab's face ever again.

And I forgot about the resident poet of my neighborhood. Until that day in the Shiraz teahouse, 16 years later.

NOW I HAD ABOUT HALF A KILO'S WORTH of Mr. Parnian's hand-written poetry in my office. I didn't know what to do with these samples. What did *he* expect me, a junior faculty member—I wasn't even in the Department of Persian Literature—to do with them? I was sure that these were original copies, and that he wanted them back eventually. I felt nervous hanging on to them. Maybe these were the only copies. He evidently didn't believe in typewriters. And photocopying wasn't easy or cheap in the early sixties in Iran. In fact, trying to reproduce written material could lead to unforeseen and sometimes troublesome situations, as I had recently found out for myself.

(To submit a paper to an American mathematical journal, I needed several clean copies of it. Having recently returned home from my studies abroad, and not quite reacclimatized to realities in Iran, I expected this to be a relatively simple task. I took my type-written original to the only copy shop in town, which still used the old *ozalid* process, the only means available at the time. After paying what I thought was an unreasonably large fee for the service, I sat down and said I would wait for my copies. "Are you kidding?" asked the proprietor of the shop, obviously surprised that I didn't know any better. "You should allow a couple of weeks at least," he explained, "because the material to be copied has to be cleared by the National Organization for Security and Information." I wondered why it would take so long for the secret police to take a look at nine pages of mathematics, given the security organization's reputation for efficiency. "Usually they require no more than a week to examine texts ready to be replicated," the man said. "But yours is almost all technical stuff. They will likely send it to their headquarters in Tehran to be examined." Lest I should take it personally, he added, "Don't forget that when the Security Organization's experts discovered the Army officers' Communist cells a few years back, they did so only by deciphering their documents written in the guise of trigonometric formulas.")

So, I couldn't return the samples to Mr. Parnian and ask for copies instead. I was hesitant to ask the poet what he wanted me to do with the collection before returning it. Surely he wouldn't be satisfied with my having "perused" the verses, as he'd put it when delivering the bundle to my office. I decided to consult Dr. Alavi, a professor of Persian literature whose office was near mine. The Faculty of Literature in Shiraz, just as in Tabriz, was still a bastion of the old guard, my poet brothers' ilk. To have a glimpse of the alternative poetry scene, you had to rely on the student groups' occasional invitations extended to modern poets, most of whom lived in the capital city, where the living was easier for them. Anyway, I figured that Shiraz provided an advantage for Mr. Parnian if he was seeking exposure to university crowds. After all, he and the Faculty of Literature here were united in their fear of the imminent demise of all rhythm and rhyme. So I knocked on my literary colleague's door with the bundle in my hand, and invited myself for a cup of tea.

"Oh, I have seen the whole lot," said Professor Alavi, as soon as he saw the samples. I had a hard time imagining the professor going through eleven kilograms of the stuff. "He is not a bad poet," he allowed, "and I myself have recommended the publication in the local papers of a few of his choice pieces. But he writes too much. And he wants to see his monumental *divan*, his oeuvre, published. In one word, he is crazy." As impartial confirmation of his assessment, the professor then whispered to me that "in fact, he was once institutionalized briefly after he quit his university studies in Tabriz, just before he moved back to his hometown here."

"I HAVE COME TO RETURN YOUR sample verses in person," I said to Mr. Parnian upon arrival at the pharmacy, where he worked. Having decided that I had to divest myself of the delicate burden, I wanted him to know that I had guarded the samples with the care they deserved. I had a suspicion that my mission, whatever it was, hadn't yet been fully accomplished, and I didn't know what else to say. He provided me with an opportunity to think it over: he invited me to tea at his home, the next day after work. I accepted.

I duly arrived with a small bunch of flowers, on account of visiting his house for the first time. It was a simple, traditional, little old house—inherited, he said, not too long ago from his late father. We sat on the carpeted floor, just as we had in his landlady's guest room in Tabriz so many years ago. Elaborate plates of fresh fruit, nuts, and cookies were already placed on the floor, over a table-cloth, in a corner of the room. I was embarrassed by the hospitality that was promising to be much more extravagant than I'd expected. Was it his nostalgia for Ali Khan Close? Was it in anticipation of possible favors from me toward the publication of his collected works? Did he really expect me to have influential friends in high places? "You don't know how much I owe your brother *Agha* Bagher and Mr. Shabestari," he said, putting me at ease, a little. "You know, it was Agha Bagher who arranged this pharmacy job for me."

The tea session was a traditional males-only affair. Which I had, of course, anticipated. His young son—the older of the two, he told me—was in charge of offering tea and treats. I had a glimpse of his chador-clad wife in the courtyard, handing the cups of hot tea on a tray to the son, who then delivered them to me and his father in the guest room. Nothing looked crazy, and any misgivings I had, resulting from my literary colleague's bold pronouncement, seemed unfounded. I allowed myself to enjoy the tranquility of the tasteful old house with the pretty little garden while we shared memories of our common Tabriz neighborhood.

"Professor Alavi likes your poetry," I said, stretching the truth a bit, desperate to find an opening for what I still thought was the inevitable topic of conversation for the afternoon. "Professor Alavi is full of himself," snapped Mr. Parnian, and then tried to be fair. "But he knows a lot about poetry, technically speaking," he said. I knew another "but" was coming, and it did, after a short pause. "But Alavi can't compose a line of verse himself if he tried." Fair enough, I thought. "He seems to be a good critic," I offered, quite sincerely this time. "No," he protested strongly, "if he were, would he promote his students' amateurish works instead of skillful, refined verses of true, talented masters? You know, we do happen to have a few of those masters amongst us in this city after all." The point was not debatable, so I changed the subject slightly. "Alavi's opinion of the new poets and modern poetry coincides with yours," I said. He conceded that the Professor's old-fashioned students were better than the best of the noisy modern poets. He was really not inter-ested in Alavi's appraisals, he said, adding that he already had made other plans for the publication of his works. Good, I thought to myself, I could perhaps relax now.

"You know," Mr. Parnian said, offering me a second piece of cake, helping himself to another piece, and motioning to his son to do likewise, "I did go back to Tabriz and revisited my old street and your Ali Khan Close." This alleviated all my anxiety about our little tea party. Nothing was required or expected of me, it was now clear, in connection with the publication of the poet's divan. Happily for me, then, this was just a renewal of acquaintance with a young man remembered by him as one perhaps capable of admiring a good old-fashioned sonnet when he heard one.

"Do you know that I met the famous poet Shahriar in Tabriz?" he asked. I knew that Shahriar had returned from Tehran, where he had acquired his fame and prominence, to the province of his birth. "Yes," he continued proudly, "Mr. Shabestari gave me the address of Shahriar's house, and I went there and knocked on his door, just like that. It was like a dream come true and, you know, old Shahriar himself opened the door, invited me in, and poured me tea with his own hands, from the teapot kept warm on the charcoal-burning brazier on the floor of his study." Totally relieved and relaxed now, I even ventured to tease him a bit: "What do you think of the fact that Shahriar has, on occasion, deviated from his classical style and written a few pieces that sound quite like modern poetry, his piece called 'Message to Einstein' for example?" Mr. Parnian had a ready answer. "Well," he said, "if just one poet were to be permitted this deviation, it should be Shahriar." He reminded me of his own old piece recited to the Ali Khan Close audience, the one in which the classical Persian poets had been resurrected to challenge the modern pretenders. "Shahriar has more than met the challenge," he continued. "He has proved his mastery in the real, time-tested, immortal art of Persian poetry. Let him have his fun with the new and transient forms if he so wishes." Mr. Parnian had another reason to offer for forgiving Shahriar's childish digressions. His eyes grew sadder and his tone changed to that of a preacher, all of a sudden. "Besides," he now confided in me, obviously referring to rumors about the famous poet's opium addiction, "one cannot discount the possible effects of certain strong drugs on the distortion of the soundest of minds." (I would be reminded of Mr. Parnian's excuse for Shahriar, two decades later, just after the 1979 Revolution: When Shahriar uncharacteristically aligned himself temporarily with the winning clerics, his admirers from among the losing political factions would find their way out of the puzzlement by citing "possible effects of opium on the soundest of minds.")

The long tea party over, I thanked Mr. Parnian and stood up to say good-by. He promised me a copy of his divan, soon to be published. I promised him a copy of my poet brother Kazem's work in return.

BY THE SUMMER OF THAT YEAR a collection of Mr. Parnian's poetry had been printed in a limited edition, thanks to the efforts of his admiring friends. He delivered three copies to me in person—the extra copies to be given to Mr. Shabestari and my brother Bagher when I next traveled to Tabriz. By picking and choosing from his voluminous work, using small font, and relegating a great number of sonnets to promised subsequent volumes, his friends had managed to reduce the weight from the frightening eleven kilos to just under one manageable kilo. (Some ambiguous pieces were also removed, he informed me in confidence, by the recommendation of the Shiraz branch of the National Organization for Security and Information. "Not that they were subversive or anything," he assured me, "but the authorities wished to prevent possible misinterpretations by potentially devious young minds.")

Late in the summer, when I visited my family in Tabriz, I delivered the books to my brother Bagher and mentioned the meeting with Mr. Parnian and his elaborate afternoon tea for me. "Mr. Parnian was very grateful to you and to Mr. Shabestari," I reported. "I suppose," I added casually, "that it was because Mr. Shabestari had shown proper appreciation of his early literary efforts, and you had, when he returned to Shiraz, introduced him to your pharmacist friend for a job." "You may suppose so," said Bagher, "I know that he is quite happy in Shiraz, with his job, his poetry, and his family."

Inevitably, the matter of Mr. Parnian's unrequited love came up. I was curious about the object of that love, Rubab, the beautiful and talented sazanda, who ended her career to marry the rich bazaar merchant. Bagher seemed to know quite a lot about the subsequent chapters of Rubab's life—which made me wonder if he had himself been romantically interested in the former musician. I now gathered from Bagher that the marriage to the rich old man from the Tabriz bazaar had come to an end by the unilateral act of a suddenly mutinous Rubab, who refused to stay in her husband's dominion once he embarked on recruiting an additional, and even younger, wife. Penniless, but resolute, Rubab returned to her mother's house. "Her prospects for a second chance were not good at all," said my brother, "until I enlisted Mr. Shabestari's help and succeeded in marrying her off again. Let me see, it must have been just after you left Tabriz to start college."

I hadn't known, I said to my brother, that he and Mr. Shabestari were that interested in Rubab's fate. Bagher gave me one of those smiles I could readily recognize since my childhood, one that prepared me for receiving a morsel of wisdom that I had regrettably neglected to imbibe while I had the opportunity. "You are so wrapped up in your mathematics," he expanded on his smile, "that you don't notice anything, do you? Who do you think the chador-clad wife in Mr. Parnian's courtyard was—the one who handed your cup of tea to her son in the courtyard?"

Showers Come to Town

The day I was banned from women's bath houses in my home city of Tabriz I wasn't quite six years old. I'd done nothing untoward, I must say right away. My mother and I had just used the facilities of the large neighborhood bath house—as we had every week, together with many other women and children—and we were just about to leave when the manager spoke. "Why don't you bring along the boy's father too, next time?" she asked Mother sternly. Mother looked embarrassed. She had to explain to me what the sarcastic question really meant. It was not a question, but an order: it was now time for me to make the big switch required of any little boy at some point; to start going to a male bath house with my father. Mother knew, of course, that a grown boy's presence among the female clientele violated the standards of public decency, but it was the definition of "grown" on which Mother didn't agree with the manager. Neither did I. A women's bath house was a fun place for kids. So, the verdict, which I knew was nonnegotiable, saddened me no end.

I have never forgotten the authoritative figure of the manager, sitting regally on what looked to me like a throne, sipping tea and ordering the workers around. Her multi-layered and multicolored dress and her elevated chair could have been the models for a painting I had seen in my household copy of the *Shahnameh,* the Book of Kings, which depicted the ancient Queen *Pourandokht* of Iran in a similar gown. And every boy and girl with access to an illustrated Shahnameh who frequented our bath house was able to see the uncanny resemblance. So we'd agreed among ourselves to refer to her as "the queen." Every customer addressed the manager as "*usta*"—a gender-free title meaning "master" or "mistress"—and treated her with respect. The throne was located prominently on one side of the spacious outer hall of the bath house, which had four large, carpeted platforms surrounding a shallow pool. The square-shaped pool looked merely decorative to the uninitiated eye, but was in fact there to serve an important ablutionary purpose toward the end of the bath house trip, when every foot would be dipped in it. Each of the four sections could easily accommodate, in addition to many kids, a dozen adult customers, who always took their time undressing and getting ready to enter the inner hall, while exchanging pleasantries with one another.

The usta's main function so far—until she pronounced the ban on my future admission—had seemed to me to be collecting money from the clients upon departure. Couldn't she have waited to break the upsetting news to Mother and me discreetly as we made our payment on our way out? But, no! She had to make such a loud announcement for the whole crowd to hear. (Mother's explanation of the biting question put to her made me think that the cruel queen was at least clever and capable of making subtle and witty remarks. But, years later, I would learn from many other former kids, male ones of course, even those who came from far-away corners of Iran, that exactly the same question, albeit in different tongues, had spelled the end of the bath-fun era for them too. The nasty queen wasn't even original, after all.)

I had every reason to be upset. I had learned from older boys that men's bath houses were very dull places indeed. But, luckily, their bath-day trips rarely lasted more than half an hour. Women's weekly bath day, on the other hand, was treated as a true social occasion. The trip was looked forward to, not least by the children, and it usually occupied a good part of the day. I should perhaps add here that the location of the public bath houses didn't change by gender, but the hours of operation did. On week days, men could use the bath houses either before daybreak or after sunset. Women and children had the whole day for themselves. But on weekends, which meant Fridays, it was men only.

Except for the very rich, who could afford to build a little bath house within their own property—in my neighborhood of two dozen homes there was just one such household in the late 1930s and early 40s—the women in Tabriz preferred to have a designated weekday for their bath-house sojourn. Ours was Tuesday. Every Tuesday our luggage for the trip was carefully prepared by Mother. It contained not only an assortment of towels and clean change of clothes, but also toiletries including body soap, face soap, foot soap, and henna; two rubbing mitts, one fine and one coarse; pumice stones for scrubbing our feet; and two portable wash basins, one of them large enough to serve as a sizable tub for a kid. It also contained a few water-proof toys for me and my playmates. And a complete cold lunch, generous enough not just to feed us, but also to make bite-size offerings to Tuesday-bath friends and acquaintances. My family did not have a live-in maid, so the task of carrying most of the luggage fell on one of the bath-house workers, for extra money and lunch. She would arrive every Tuesday after breakfast to accompany us to the bath house, and back home again sometime in the afternoon.

Upon arrival at the bath house, clients would be directed by the usta's hand motions to a vacant spot on one of the four platforms of the outer hall for preparations before entering the equally spacious and impressive, domed inner hall, the hot bath house proper. Their dirty and clean clothes, separately parceled and marked for easy recognition later, would be left on the wide shelves around the walls of the outer hall, awaiting their reemergence in four or five hours. The preliminary greetings and small talk with the neighbors in the outer hall over, and the undressing done, Mother and I would put on our bathing suits before proceeding to the inner hall. Mother's bathing suit, like every other woman's, was a bath-towel-sized piece of thin, dark, nonabsorbent material, called "*fita*" in the local tongue, specially manufactured for the purpose. The wealthier clients owned very fine, imported fitas, but the domestically woven variety was of course more common and quite as functional. The fita was wrapped around the lower body, above the knees. My optional fita, like every other little kid's, was a cheaper, miniature version of the real thing, made at home. Everybody was topless. Except for the queen, who was fully dressed, even when she entered the inner hall for a random inspection.

Once inside the main hall, the pace got even more leisurely. It seemed that nobody was ever in a hurry to bathe, get dressed, and go home. The air in the hall was pleasantly hot and steamy. Each group of family or close friends filled their large basin with water and sat around it, relaxing and chatting, lazily allowing their nearly naked bodies to "soak" in the hot, humid air—a process deemed necessary for physical cleansing. If they had smeared their hair or their hands with a dye, they had to wait for it to work properly before washing; sometimes for hours. All beautifying activities took place openly, often communally, except hair removal, for which there was a private annex admitting one adult at a time. So the waiting line to enter it provided another welcome opportunity for chatting and making new friends. The children played with their water toys, and they bombarded each other and selected grownups with soap bubbles. If a woman spotted a friend or acquaintance sitting in another circle, she stealthily approached her from behind with a can of lukewarm water in hand, and surprised her by gently pouring water on her shoulder. Greetings, pleasantries, and exchange of latest news followed. If you made a habit of neglecting this symbolic assistance with the ablutions of an acquaintance, and if you consistently allowed yourself to be a sitting target for similar salutations, you were definitely showing unwelcome signs of self-importance.

This social occasion for women and children was like no other. At any other meeting of women, there was always the likely sudden appearance on the scene of a man or a teenage boy, which would make it necessary for a woman to cover not just her body, but also her hair and most of her face. Even in formal religious gatherings of women, the presiding preacher would usually be a man, so you couldn't even see the full faces of the other women present until the man left, allowing for a brief tea break before the next male preacher arrived. So here, at this weekly meeting in the bath house, a fully man-free sanctuary, a woman had her rare opportunity to feel truly unencumbered. And she cherished it. (Years later, I would be puzzled by how the proverbial Persian expression "women's bath house" was frequently used by men to refer to an extremely noisy place. My recollection was quite the opposite: Unlike men's public tea houses, scenes of loud arguments and sometimes rowdy behavior, a female bath house—women's answer to the all-male tea house—was calm and serene. Even the kids in our bath house had always behaved themselves, unless my memory is being selective here. Or, perhaps, our queen wasn't a typical usta; perhaps she had ruled with an iron fist.)

And it was here, in the women's bath house, that you could eye potential brides for your eligible sons, brothers, or nephews. View them *au naturel*, almost. With very little to hide. Even if you didn't have eligible male relatives yourself, you used the occasion to do the eyeing for your friends and neighbors. I heard many an oral report exchanged among my mother's friends after a bath house trip. They were usually generous, and mostly about beautiful, healthy skin. The only negative evaluations I remember hearing were, "She is a little pale in the face," or "She is a little too skinny." But the comments usually had an optimistic ending: "Not that it couldn't be easily remedied."

It was in this female public square, as well, that elaborate, prenuptial "bridal baths" took place. A bridal bath, attended by the bride's family and friends, wasn't just a time-honored ceremony. An equally important purpose of it was to make the young bride, almost always in her mid-teens, as beautiful as humanly possible. And to spoil her silly, before shipping her to the groom's household, where she would face her new adult duties under the supervision of her in-laws—who, the bride's family prayed and hoped, would be as kind and understanding as appearances had indicated. Occasional beautification tips on, say, what balm should be applied to the bride's lips, how much of her eyebrow hair should be removed, or how dark the remainder of the eyebrows should be made to look, came from every friendly corner of the bath hall. Not just from the members of the bride's retinue, but also from the rest of the well-meaning bath house attendees. Families with large bridal parties, who could afford it, booked the whole bath house for most of the day. This was very disappointing for us if the day happened to be a Tuesday (and if we were not included in the guest list): No packed lunch, no relaxed chats, and no extended play time for the kids. The bath trip was shortened and postponed to late afternoon. We had to get in and out in just a couple of hours. "There was no time to soak, even" would be the consensus among the disgruntled clients leaving the bath house in a hurry, before sunset, in time to make room for the male clients of the day.

Each working woman on duty in the bath house was specialized in one of several jobs. Quite a few of them were there just to help you with the general scrubbing and washing. Some gave you hair and skin treatments. The most experienced workers gave you therapeutic massages, especially sought by elderly clients. Each service had a set fee. Every worker knew your name. She also memorized what services she had performed for you and your party, so she could later help the usta figure the amount on the final bill, so to speak. There was no actual bill, of course; the workers couldn't read or write. Neither could the queen, although she seemed to be proficient with her handy abacus.

To ruin my day, the queen had chosen a happy occasion, when I had especially enjoyed my play time with the bath-house friends. This day marked the ending of an unprecedented, very inconvenient, hiatus in our regular, weekly trips to the bath house. This situation, out of everybody's hands, had lasted a couple of months. It was bearable only because it occurred in summertime, which made it possible to perform ablutions in backyards or basements, albeit with considerable difficulty. It had all started in the late spring with the closure of bath houses, leading to that unforgettable summer.

"The bath house is closed, locked and sealed," announced Lady Bagim urgently, as soon as my mother opened our front door to let her in. Lady Bagim was a dear old neighbor who came for a short visit almost every day. This morning she looked very worried. She had just seen it with her own eyes, she said, the shut-and-sealed gate of our neighborhood bath house. It was by the Shah's orders, she said. If she could read the signs on the walls, she would have known, as did my father, that the closure was ordered by the Department of Health. Every public bath house was now required to be equipped with individual showers. Lady Bagim was horrified that the conventional *khazna*, the huge hot tub in the bath house that could hold a dozen clients at a time, was now condemned as unsanitary. The khasna, used thus far by all bath-goers for their final bodily cleansing by immersion, had been such an essential part of the public bath house for centuries, perhaps millennia, that its demise was unthinkable for most of the citizenry. Now every one of these facilities had to stay closed unless and until it was converted to a modern one with individual showers. Lady Bagim knew this was coming, as did everyone else. But she had hoped that a certain important religious issue would be resolved first: whether showers were adequate for the ritual cleansing that was of great importance to every pious man and woman. Mosques and bath houses in Iran did not only represent two of the most striking parts of every city's traditional architecture. Both were also of great importance for the total purification, in body and soul, of a pious adult. Pious adults would not set foot in a mosque, nor venture to say their mandatory prayers without proper ablutions. Proper ablutions in several circumstances, say, after sexual intercourse, or at the end of a menstrual cycle, or after touching any part of a dead body, couldn't be performed without a complete, ritual body wash, which necessitated, certainly in wintertime, an urgent trip to a bath house.

Anxiety and panic ruled the traditional family lives in Tabriz that summer. It came in varying degrees, depending on the opinion of each family's particular "source of emulation" or "model for imitation." This term referred to a distinguished and certified cleric picked by the head of the household. Each such source issued a specific religious edict—a *fatwa*, to use a word that is perhaps quite familiar nowadays—on everything that concerned the everyday life of every member of his congregation. Such an edict was supposed to be followed verbatim. According to some sources of emulation, including the one followed by Lady Bagim's family, showers presented a difficult problem. They had to be assumed inadequate for cleansing, pending further studies. Thus Lady Bagim would be deprived of proper ablutions for several months. My family's source of emulation had, luckily, approved of shower-equipped facilities early in the game. And I had actually looked forward to using them, not just for the novelty of the thing, but mainly because I found the traditional Khazna not fun at all, unlike everything else connected with the bath house. It was usually either too hot or too cold for my taste. Immersing in it was of course an obligatory, but luckily very brief, finale to the weekly bath trip.

So it was with great pleasure that Mother and I were visiting the newly remodeled bath house. On my first khazna-free bath day, I thoroughly enjoyed the comfort of the just-installed showers with miraculously controllable water temperature. It was a happy day. Until it ended by the queen's orders. Mother had expected a large crowd during this particular week, on account of the lengthy bath house closure preceding it. But it turned out that quite a few customers were still staying away, evidently waiting for their families' sources of emulation, their chosen leaders, to come up with a final statement on the suitability of shower water for cleansing.

I MUST DIGRESS HERE TO RECORD the correct definition of certain terms; this is of paramount importance to the appreciation of the ritual cleansing rules to be followed by the faithful. The rules which apply, for example, if a hand or a foot has touched something unclean: urine, blood, alcohol, wet hair of a dog; the list cannot be exhausted here. One must learn, as early as possible in one's life, how to use water for cleansing. You, Dear Reader, can skip to the end of this long paragraph if you are conversant with the term "*Kurr.*" Otherwise, here comes the necessary explanation. For the ritual washing by water, you have to know what kind of water it is you are dealing with. The water has to be pure and clean, of course. Now, if it is a very limited amount, such as a quantity contained in a vessel or a watering can, then you should pour it on the contaminated object or body part. Three consecutive times, to be on the safe side. Each time with a continuous flow. If it is running water, such as a river or a brook you are lucky to have access to, you can just dip the object or body part in it; preferably three times. But if you have to use "dormant," or non-running water for this method, that is, cleansing by dipping, then you have to make sure the amount of water exceeds a certain volume I am coming to, shortly. Otherwise the dipping will not only fail to cleanse, but will also contaminate the water itself and render it useless. There is no problem if you have an easily reachable lake, pond, or pool. But if it is a tubful of water you have to make do with, there is an absolute minimum, called "Kurr." This is quite unambiguously defined, in most books treating the subject: it is the volume of a cube each of whose sides measures three and a half *spans*. A span, or a hand span, is the distance from the tip of your thumb to the tip of your little finger, fully stretched. Assuming of course that you are an adult. Now an "answer book" authorized by a prominent scholar, a source worthy of emulation, may give a metric value for the kurr, for the benefit of the more modern members of his flock. The values I've checked in some of these books range from 377 to 483 liters, with some baffling estimates recorded to three decimal points. The authors cannot be blamed, of course, for having large or small hands, or, alternatively, for making the convenient assumption that all adult hands were created equal. I also checked the Oxford English Dictionary for "span" as a measure of length. Sure enough, it is there: a span is supposed to equal nine inches. But this gives more than 560 liters for a proper kurr. Not consistent with the amounts prescribed in the books by the real authorities. Perhaps it would be prudent of the folk at the Oxford English Dictionary to change their definition of "span" from nine to eight inches. The least they could do, in the name of world peace.

Okay, we are there, finally: I am done with the absolutely necessary technicalities. You are now fully ready to appreciate the goings-on in the pious circles of Tabriz during that summer of discontent, more than seventy years ago, which started with the bath-house closures and ended with my last trip to the women's bath house. The potential calamity that Lady Bagim together with a legion of pious citizens, male and female, were facing that summer was enormous. Unless, of course, the scholars of the Faith could come up with a solution to the ablution problem: In which category of clean water, if any, could one place what was coming out of those foreign-looking showerheads? And was it really adequate for a proper cleansing? Taking a shower was certainly not immersion in water, your preferred method made possible by the old khazna. So the kurr designation wouldn't apply to these modern devices. But what about the running-water or pouring-from-a-vessel methods? There seemed to be no consensus among the scholars, several of whom were still unable to find a way out. Some of them advised their respective flocks to exercise extreme caution and, if possible, make alternative washing arrangements for the time being. These warnings, which were of course dispensed underground, were circulated by word of mouth—for fear of retaliation by the formidable Shah's police. The purists among the clergy hadn't forgotten what happened some five years earlier, in the mid-thirties, when the secularizing and modernizing policies of the monarch, especially his obligatory dress codes, had infuriated the custodians of the True Faith. On that occasion the protests by their stubborn followers, gathered in a sacred mosque in northeastern Iran, had been put down brutally by the Shah's men, and resulted in many, some said hundreds of, deaths.

According to the particular cleric my family and several of our neighbors emulated, it was permitted, thank God, to treat the water emanating from the modern showerheads as if it were running water. You just had to make sure that there was a strong enough flow of water. "If it could be described as trickling," our source warned us, "it was no good." Apparently, what saved the novel method for cleansing was the fact that the shower was connected to, not just one, but two large kurr sources: there was the hot water source, the former khazna, still there but now off limits to clients; and there was the cold water source, the huge storage tank attached to the bath house. They certainly qualified as kurrs a hundred times over, according to my family's source. You were out of luck, however, if your family emulated a cleric with an opposite opinion. Some sources of emulation took months to study the relevant facts and come up with a final affirmative verdict. (Rumors had it that in certain cases the police had a hand in persuading them.)

"I wish we had moved back to our village of birth," said Lady Saria the Pious, our most devout neighbor. She had just reluctantly used a shower-equipped facility. "My late husband, God bless his soul, was all for leaving the city," she reminisced. "You know, he wanted us to go back six years ago, not too long before he died; you know, the time the Shah started to talk about banning women's headscarves. My husband, bless his soul, was right. The Shah's police never got to enforce his evil laws in small towns. Those women who moved away from the big city were lucky. They never had to bare their faces and heads in public. They were simply ignored by the Shah, you know. They didn't count, as far as the Shah was concerned." Lady Saria had just learned from her relatives in the village that they were spared again, and there was no talk of converting their clean khaznas to those dubious shower stalls. She was typical of the people who finally started to make use of the new method for sacred ablutions, but reluctantly. They felt that they were compromising something, somewhere, somehow. Even after their sources of emulation had finally and formally approved of the foreign practice.

Not long after showers came to town, Tabriz would be occupied by the Russians in 1941, and the old Shah would be forced by the Allies to abdicate in favor of his young son (who ruled as the last Shah of Iran before the 1979 Revolution). Lady Saria the pious and Lady Bagim would be elated that the new Shah's police could no longer enforce the emancipation laws, and that women could once again fully cover themselves in public, if they so chose. Men's dress codes would also go unenforced. Clerics would start to announce their fatwas openly now that their detested monarch was gone. They would be particularly, and unanimously, unforgiving of bare-headed women. Curiously, however, they would refrain from condemning bath house showers. The khazna would never be revived, and the shower would be there to stay. Perhaps because of the forbidding costs of any reconversion during the war time and in the foreign-occupied city. This was all in the near future, while the modernizing Shah still ruled absolutely— for the time being.

SO, THIS WAS IT FOR ME. I was now considered a man at the age of six, at least for bathing purposes. Father would wake me up very early in the morning on a day that seemed random to me at the time, but was of course dictated by his own ablutionary requirements. And we would take a fast walk in pitch darkness to our bath house, the same one I had frequented with Mother. The place now looked drab and dull. The male usta did not look or behave like a king at all. The male clients did exchange greetings when they arrived at the outer hall, but that was pretty much it until they said goodbye on the way out. We undressed quickly, put on our fitas—supplied by the bath house, not brought from home—and entered the hot inner hall in a matter of minutes. No kid seemed to be enjoying himself in the bath house. Not that there was time for boys to play or even talk to each other. Only male kids were allowed, of course. There was no soaking time to speak of. We scrubbed, washed, showered, and left. We were home before sunrise, in time for Father to say his morning prayers before it was too late.

Get used to it, I told myself. This was men's version of the bath day. It was a serious task, a duty, not a game. I would keep wondering, though, why men didn't use the occasion for socialization the way women did. I would learn nearly ten years later, when I was able to read the Persian classics, that bath trips were different for at least some men in the old days. (One tale would impress me deeply enough to be etched in my memory: It was about a meeting of two historic personalities who lived a thousand years before our time. One was the world-famous Ibn-Sina, otherwise known as Avicenna, the philosopher, scientist, and physician. The other was Abusa'id, an icon of Persian sufism. They couldn't be more different in their worldviews. They were celebrated members of opposite camps in the eternal war between science and mysticism; between the objective and the subjective; between the temporal and the spiritual. A grandson of Abusa'id's wrote a whole book on the spiritual visions the great mystic had, the miracles he performed, and the words of wisdom he uttered. One day, the grandson reports in the book, these two learned giants of the warring camps meet—the author is clearly proud of the contribution he is making toward a potential rapprochement between the enemies. The two men go to the bath house and engage in a deep conversation, deep enough to last three full days. When they finally reemerge, they are interviewed, separately, by certain of their respective followers on the outcomes of the obviously important discourse. They are both brief and brilliant with their independent responses, which the book records, and which so unforgettably impresses the teenage me: "What I see, he knows," says the visionary mystic. "What I know, he sees," says the great philosopher. How profound could learned men get?)

MORE THAN TWO YEARS had passed since my exile from women's bath houses. My second-grade classmate Firuz and I were doing our school assignments together at his home. (His house, one of the richest and most modern I had ever visited, did have its own private bath and shower—actually inside the building, and not on the far side of the backyard. Firuz's mother was one of the very few mothers I knew who could read and write. His father, a supervisor in the Federal Tax Bureau, had spent time in France. The family was, in short, *Frangi-ma'ab*—that is, one with Western lifestyle.) Firuz and I had been instructed to pick a short poem each and memorize it, to be recited in class. His father had taken us into his large study-library and picked a few easy poetry books suitable for young children. Having suggested some poems from the books, he'd left us to our own devices. The size of his library and the books whose titles I couldn't read, and I assumed to be in French, were awe-inspiring. But what truly fascinated me was a painting on the wall.

The painting definitely depicted women in a bath house, I thought to myself. The women looked exactly like those I used to be allowed to see every Tuesday. They seemed to be attending to their washing and cleaning chores as if no strange men were around to watch them. They were perhaps exchanging recipes or neighborhood news. But somebody in the bath house had obviously studied their figures very carefully to be able to sketch them. It couldn't be an easy job at all. While Firuz and I memorized our chosen pieces from a cute little book about cats, I couldn't take my eyes off the painting, or my mind off all those fun Tuesdays of yore.

Firuz's dad returned to his study to reward us with some candy. "*If,*" he said, raising an index finger in mock severity. "If you have your pieces already memorized." We said we had, and he trusted us. He noticed my fascination with the painting on the wall. "So, you like pictures of nude ladies," he said with a smile. He looked like a grownup who would allow himself a conversation with a mere kid. I was emboldened to ask questions, and I asked many. My own memory of the conversation is vague, perhaps because it ended with his amused laughter that embarrassed me. Here I'll have to rely on the later reminiscences by this kindly man, Firuz's enviable father, who never tired of teasing me about the exchange, even years later, when Firuz and I were both university students:

"Who painted this pictures, Mr. Burumand?"

"This is a copy, Son. The original painting is by a Frenchman named Renoir."

"How old is this Renoir?"

"Gone, I am afraid. Passed away many years ago."

"How old was Renoir at the time?"

"At the time of painting? I suppose 50 or 60. Why?"

"Was Renoir a man or a woman?"

"A man. Why?"

"You mean, in France they allow grown men into women's bath houses?"

Faulty Forecasts

My old neighbor Lady Bagim had an extra-ordinary dream about Adolf Hitler. "The German king" she called him as she excitedly related her dream to my mother. It must have been a late-winter day in 1943—according to my later calculations. Mother had taken me along to visit Lady Bagim, who was recovering from some ailment, still in bed. I was eight years old and quite comfortable with the designation "king" for both Hitler and Stalin. Everything I knew about them or about world affairs in general I had learned from my father and his friends, who seemed to be discussing the ongoing Battle of Stalingrad every time they met. Their information came mostly from newspapers. A couple of them also owned radio sets—radio was still a novelty in Iran at the time— which they could tune in to the Persian-language news from abroad. Radio Moscow was readily accessible, but Radio Berlin only with considerable difficulty—the Russian forces occupying northern Iran at the time were evidently jamming German broadcasts.

Lady Bagim's dream had involved more than just the king of Germany. In fact, the main personage in the dream was her favorite Saint, the revered Hidden Imam, the Twelfth Infallible Imam, who had disappeared in the tenth century, and whose reappearance had ever since been longed and prayed for by every pious man and woman I knew. "May God expedite my Master's reappearance," said Lady

Bagim, uttering a common prayer. "His image in my dream was so clear and unmistakable. You couldn't see my Master's face, of course, so bright was the halo of light surrounding his blessed head. He was sitting on his high throne on a mountaintop, pointing to this man standing next to him he called 'Heydar'…"

I perked up once I heard my own name mentioned in Lady Bagim's dream. Lady Bagim, apparently oblivious to my personal interest in the matter, went on. "The man was standing at attention to my Master's right—a big man wearing a *Frangi* suit, a necktie, and a chapeau. Clean-shaven except for his mustache. 'You may know this man only as a king, king of Germany,' My Master was saying, 'you may even think that he is a *kafar*, an infidel. But I know better, and I am telling you: he has seen the light. He has converted to the Right Path. Do not judge him by his suit and tie or by his bald-shaven face. He hasn't yet revealed his true faith and real name to the world—on account of his own subjects still being infidels. As soon as he defeats the godless Bolsheviks in Russia, he will tell the whole world what his real name is: Heydar and not Hitler.' Then my Master, may God expedite his return, gave us the good news: 'The End of Time, and my own reappearance just before that, won't be long now,' he said. 'But, in my temporary absence, this man to my right, Heydar, is my deputy on Earth. Obey him as you would obey me.' "

Wow! Could it be true? I'd heard from grownups that pious people's dreams often came true. In fact, Lady Bagim's own recently deceased husband, who was known to have lived long and piously, "under six Persian kings," as he used to put it proudly, was fond of telling everyone about his own true dreams in the past: He had dreamed, he often boasted, of the demise of each of the last five Shahs of Iran, many nights before each event. A true dream could always count as one proof of the dreamer's piety. And Lady Bagim was certainly one of the most pious ladies on the block. Perhaps second only to Lady Saria the Pious, my other neighbor, and my best friend's grandmother. Together with her husband, Lady Bagim had made several pilgrimages to the holy shrines in Iran and Iraq, and distributed alms to the poor after each round. So, I couldn't stop thinking about the dream, even after Mother and Lady Bagim changed topics several times and consumed many cups of tea.

THE TWELFTH IMAM WAS, in my mind, the most important holy figure after God Himself. I knew this from a personal experience going back a couple of years: It happened on a summer day, a few weeks before I started elementary school—the exact date, as I would learn later, was August 25, 1941—the day the Russians came to Tabriz. Suddenly, the sky filled with warplanes that morning. For a few moments Father thought it was a routine exercise by the Royal Iranian Air Force. But soon the number of the planes exceeded what father estimated to be the total number possessed by the nation's armed forces. Then we heard horrible sounds from every direction. Sounds of explosion. A neighbor, one of the only two on the block who owned radio sets, knocked on our door and told us to seek a safe shelter. Our large basement was judged to be the oldest and most solidly built in our cul-de-sac. So several neighbors came over, and they brought their mattresses, pillows, and comforters. They stayed for three days and nights. There must have been about a dozen of them. I was the only kid in the desperate crowd, which was not in itself a cause of worry for me—as a kid, I seemed to enjoy the company of adults more than my friends did.

For three days we kept hearing the horrible sounds of bombs dropped from the Russian airplanes. We held our breaths each time, in case one of them exploded in our backyard. In constant fear, we waited and prayed for the bombardment to stop. Our kitchen was connected to the basement, thank God. So we didn't have to come out of the building except to run to the outhouse, which was on the far side of the yard. Everybody said more prayers than usual, especially when in the open, out of the basement. Some prayers were directed toward the Almighty Himself, of course, but most of them addressed intermediaries, that is, His representatives on Earth: the Martyrs of the Faith, the twelve Infallible Imams. Each man and woman favored one or other of the ancient saints. I, however, kept invoking the Twelfth Imam's name exclusively. I knew why, by my six-year-old logic: After all, this last Imam was the only one still alive, and thus readier and more available to help than the ones in Heaven. If only I could get his attention. "O the Twelfth Imam, save us please!" I kept pleading aloud, without mentioning his real name. I'd learned from my elders that it was disrespectful to address him audibly as "Mahdi" without proper ablutions, or before standing up first, if you were sitting.

"DELIRIUM!" EXCLAIMED MOTHER, when I asked questions about Lady Bagim's dream as soon as we left her home. "It was a fever dream. The Hidden Imam doesn't need Hitler's or any other infidel's help, even if they rename themselves after our Imams to fool us; even if they pretend to be true converts. The Hidden Imam will appear when the time is ripe, with God's own permission." But I wasn't quite satisfied. I decided to consult my older brother Bagher.

Just over twenty years old at the time, Bagher had left Tabriz to attend college in the capital city, but was now at home for a short visit. Several family friends were having tea with him at our house when mother and I returned from Lady Bagim's. They all started to laugh out loud when I told them about the dream that had so impressed me. Quite a few big words were used in the ensuing conversation which were beyond my comprehension. I only got the gist of some of what was said. One fellow seemed to be saying that the dream wasn't original or unusual at all. "The Nazi propaganda machine is responsible for all this," he said. "My own mother is also an admirer of the super-human leader of Germany who will defeat Communist Russia. She is hoping, among other things, that all those old, worthless Russian Ruble notes from the late Tsar's time she has saved for years and years will soon be redeemable, and that we will be as rich as we once were!" This fancy talk, while not really comprehensible to me, certainly explained Lady Bagim's recently acquired reluctance to give away her own useless Russian-Tsar coins. Until very recently, she had always generously supplied the neighborhood kids, including me and her own grandson, with all the play money we needed.

Had her new dream perhaps included a promise of regained value for her old coin collection?

The grown-up conversation reminded me of my rich schoolmate Behnam's recent report whispered to me. I now whispered it to my brother. "Behnam's father must have some old Russian money too," I conjectured, "because he says his father loves Hitler so much that he's had a swastika built into the brickwork right above the front door of their home. Behnam says it is done so cleverly that no one can possibly notice it." My brother, who knew and disliked Behnam's father, relayed the story to the whole tea party with a mixture of amusement and disgust. "This guy is a lot subtler than a similar rich old fellow I know," said a guest. "He has a German flag hidden in his house, waiting for the German Army to come to Iran and kick the Russians out." The conversation switched to the Battle of Stalingrad. "You'll soon have lots of old Tsar money to play with," an older guest promised me confidently, and then turned to address the grownups in their own fancy language again. Here is how I now approximate what he said: "The idea in Lady Bagim's dream of secret conversion of world leaders to the Right Faith goes back many years," he said, reminiscing about World War I. "Kaiser Wilhelm, sometimes presented to the Moslem world as 'Hajj Wilhelm,' also posed as one who had seen the light and secretly made his dutiful pilgrimage to Mecca. And he did actually try to mobilize the faithful in the Middle East for a sacred war, a jihad, against the British Empire." Then another guest, a younger man, started to say something about the Twelfth Imam. It was going to be blasphemous, I guessed, because he stopped in mid-sentence as soon as my father came home and joined the gathering for tea.

LADY BAGIM'S DREAM OR DELIRIUM, whichever it was, had combined two seemingly very different topics I was hearing about these days, almost everywhere I went. The world war in progress was one, of course. But the imminent reappearance of the Hidden Imam was a more frequent topic of conversation with the devout citizens of Tabriz. Especially while they attended their regular religious gatherings, held separately for men and women. These "*marsia*" sessions, had been classified as superstitious activities and banned by the old Shah of Iran. Until he was sent to exile in 1941 by the Allies. Kept alive as underground affairs for several years, these sessions had now resurfaced and were proliferating—thanks, ironically, to the occupation of the province by "infidel Bolsheviks." Marsia participants traditionally listened first to a brief and usually perfunctory sermon by a preacher. Then they mourned with him the martyrdom of a selected saint and his loyal followers. Of particular interest were the Third Infallible Imam and his companions, murdered in Iraq in the seventh century. The marsia also included urgent pleas to the Twelfth Infallible Imam to end his long absence and to come out of what has been termed his Major Occultation. In later years, I would learn about a remarkable coincidence that must have played a role in this extreme preoccupation of my pious compatriots during those war years, especially right after 1941: the Major Occultation had, according to the reliable chroniclers of the miraculous life of the Hidden

Imam, taken place precisely a thousand years before the Allied occupation of Iran. In the year 941 A.D.

My grandmother once took me to one of those marsia sessions. The presiding preacher, the only man present (except for "innocent" little boys like me, accompanying female participants) was sternly waving a thick book at the congregation. Its hefty title was "Harbingers of the Revelation," he said. It listed hundreds of sure signs of the Last Coming. All those terrible things that were supposed to happen just a little before the End of Time. He proceeded to read selected paragraphs from the book, prefacing each item with "It is written that… ."

I should pause here to say that "It is written that" was the standard shorthand for an informal reference to a document presumed to be reliable. The more scholarly form of this kind of reference would start, more or less, like this: "Scholar A relates from Scholar B, who heard in person from the Sixth Infallible Imam himself that . . ." Here A and B would come from a list of trustworthy sources recognizable to, and respected by, the theologically sophisticated. For the uneducated masses, it sufficed to hear from somebody they trusted that "it was written."

"Here is one," the preacher said, "it is written that food and coal will be scarce and expensive just before our Master reveals himself. Now who can tell me that it hasn't happened already?" He had a point: even I, just a young kid, had to agree that it had: Wasn't bread rationed in my own city now? Wasn't my mother using dried apple peels to make a tea substitute for the family, and saving the pricey, hard-to-come-by, real tea for our guests? Weren't Lady Bagim and

Lady Saria collecting money from other pious women to buy charcoal to distribute among our poorer neighbors for winter heating? The preacher was going on with a seemingly endless list of prophecies from the book he was holding, and every one of them seemed to have been fulfilled already. Certainly there was war almost everywhere in the world now, for another predicted sign. Disease was rampant, as the book on display had accurately foreseen, and as I could personally attest to. My brother had just survived a pre-penicillin, war-time outbreak of typhoid. To guard against the dreaded typhus epidemic, I was myself wearing a medicinal necklace all the time. So did all my schoolmates. Dangling from each of these necklaces was a small metal container filled with henna to hold in place a drop of mercury. The mercury was supposed to deflect body lice which carried the typhus germ.

"And what about all those indecent women out there in the open?" the preacher asked triumphantly, picking yet another item from the book of signs he was waving at us, which reconfirmed his belief in the fast-approaching end of time. "Those shameless women with exposed hair and made-up faces you encounter every day, God help them atone for their sins." His fear of the women he called indecent seemed genuine. He really wanted the audience to avoid them at any cost; and he offered helpful hints for identifying them further: "You know the type: they are *not* like you; they show no fear of God whatsoever; they socialize with men freely; they even shake hands with men—and I don't mean only the men in their own family either. May the Almighty save all of us men from their Satanic temptations."

I didn't quite understand why exposed hair or uncovered face of a woman was a bad thing, but my grandmother assured me that I was still too young to understand. She said I would see clearly one day, after I grew up, how indecent and sinful it was for a woman to bare her hair in public or to shake hands with men. (The day never came, by the way: Not when I was in elementary school, an all-boys establishment which made exceptions for the owner-principal's own daughter and her best female friend who both exposed their hair and face for everyone to see. Not when I started to notice, on the way to my high school, the pretty school girls with uncovered faces. Not when our few "liberated" female relatives—as Mother used to call them—came to visit, and did not cover their hair unless Father was home. Not when I encountered bare-haired female classmates in college. And not even this morning of October 5, 2015, before I started to write the current paragraph, when I learned, while checking the latest Iranian news on the Internet, that a handshake in a Tehran prison between a female inmate and her male defense attorney has just resulted in formal charges of indecency against them both.)

Lady Saria the Pious was even more enthusiastic than Lady Bagim as an advocate of preparations for the Great Reappearance. Together, they organized tea sessions for the neighborhood women in which they said special, lengthy prayers to urge the Imam to come back. To come back and put an end to the prevailing and widespread injustice on Earth, and reward the faithful, as promised. They seemed to be asking the Imam urgently, perhaps a little too boldly, "What are you waiting for, now that the evidence, all piled up, is there for everyone to see?" One participant in these prayer sessions was overly frightened by Lady Saria's predictions of the imminent Last Coming, especially when she heard about Lady Bagim's dream. Lady Saria was moved to console her. "Don't worry," she said to her, "but pray for forgiveness before it is too late." The woman didn't seem to be satisfied. "I am not the one," she said. "I'm not the one who is sinning. It is my son, and I can't stop him. He has joined this group of singers and violin players in his school—they call it their music club—and he says that when he grows up, he hopes to join an *orgester* and sing on the radio. What will happen to him when our Master comes and starts to punish the sinners?" Lady Saria could only hope for the son to stop these activities in time. "But I told you what to do last summer," she reminded the woman helpfully, "and it is not too late yet. Just take him out of this government school run by infidels! You know, there are good private schools available now, God be thanked. They allow no sinful activities in these schools, and the students are taught only what is right." The mother sighed. "If only I could persuade his father," she said. Lady Saria acknowledged the problem, but didn't give up all hope. "There is still some time to repent for the sinners," she said to the desperate mother. "Not every sign of the Final Appearance is quite there yet, anyway." "What signs? What other signs?" several curious members of the audience wanted to know, trusting Lady Saria's expertise. "For one thing," replied Lady Saria with her usual self-confidence, "it is written that before our Master's coming, the new moon will bend in the sky like a thin twig until its two ends meet. It is also written that a star brighter than the full Moon will appear in the night sky."

One young member of the congregation grew impatient with the conversation. She asked Lady Saria a question about the Hidden Imam that even I, a mere kid, knew was impertinent: "How can a man live more than a thousand years?" Saria didn't seem as shocked by the question as some of the other women and I were, and proceeded to enlighten the questioner. "But, my dear, this is not an ordinary man," she informed her. "Besides, there have been other instances of extra-long life whenever the Almighty willed it. Don't you remember from your Scripture lessons about Noah, peace be upon him? Don't you know that his prophecy lasted for 950 years?—Or don't they have time for these lessons in the kind of school you girls attend these days? Now, take 950 and add to it Prophet Noah's age at the time he was chosen by the Almighty to be His messenger on Earth. Or, for another example, think of Khizr, the prophet who, as we all know, is still alive, and walking amongst us unrecognized. He was born even before Moses, peace be upon him. How old would he be now? Let us see. Well over 3000 years, wouldn't you say?" The young woman didn't seem to have any further questions at this time.

IT TOOK A SUICIDE ON HITLER'S PART to convince Lady Bagim that her dream about the Fuhrer had indeed been a false one, the kind of dream to which not even the most pious among us were always immune. When the war ended, she was finally sure that the Tsars weren't coming back. She once again opened her purse of old Russian coins, and even unearthed some beautifully illustrated and sturdy pre-Revolution Russian banknotes for the kids to play with. Behnam's father categorically denied the existence of a hidden swastika in the brickwork above the entrance to his home, and challenged any of his doubters to prove him wrong.

LINKING THE AFFAIRS OF THE Hidden Imam to those of live, unhidden politicians on the world stage went out of fashion for a while—and would stay that way pretty much for several decades, at least in Iran, while the last Shah ruled over a pseudo-secular state. But a quarter century after the 1979 Revolution, President Ahmadinejad of the Islamic Republic of Iran would take a very personal interest in the imminent Reappearance. He would name his cabinet after the Twelfth Imam, and would, in his formal address to the United Nations General Assembly in 2005, include an appeal to the Almighty to hasten the long-awaited event. His government would also turn a small shrine in the village of Jamkaran, not too far from the capital city (built on the site of a water well at which the Holy Hidden Imam is said to have revealed himself to a select few on a Tuesday) into a major center for pilgrimage. The site would prove popular, and tens of thousands of the faithful would gather there every day, even more on Tuesdays. They would come to pray. To donate money. To deposit their requests in writing, addressed to the Hidden Imam himself, in the sacred well, now especially remodeled for the purpose. And, weather permitting, to enjoy a family picnic on the extensive grounds of the shrine.

This was all still in the distant future, of course, while I attended my "modern" school, so frowned upon by Lady Saria. So was the "Scientific approach" to the Reappearance question—as opposed to just simple references to documented pronouncements in reliable books. These scientific studies would find followers worldwide. In 2009, for example, meticulous "numerical analysis" performed by a learned gentleman in Indonesia would result in his unequivocal announcement of the exact date of October 23, 2015 for the Return of the Twelfth Imam. Also, an ambitious freelance scholar in Iran, a young professor at the "research institute" founded by himself, would publish the results of an exact calculation of his. Of the 1200 signs of the Imminent Coming, all but five have already occurred, he would warn the sinners among his television audience.

Another thing still in the future was the proliferation of daring individuals claiming to be the promised Hidden Imam finally revealed in the flesh. Their numbers—hitherto few and far between—would swell in Iran during the late twentieth and early twenty-first centuries. This in spite of the severe punishments for false claimants surely to be antic-ipated, given the no-nonsense approach of the new regime toward all matters religious. A 2013 report in the journal Economist would quote an Iranian source as saying, "More than three thousand fake Twelfth Imams are currently serving various prison terms in Iran."

MEANWHILE, AS I WENT THROUGH elementary school, forecasts kept coming slowly, but steadily. Dedicated harbingers of the Last Coming were perhaps a little disappointed that all the world calamities, wars, genocides, diseases, and famines had been false alarms. But they never gave up hope. "It is written that" continued to be a favorite opening, especially with Lady Saria—to guarantee the authenticity of quotations from various saints and their dedicated representatives. My school years produced only sporadic cases of individuals claiming to be the returning Imam in the flesh. Most were ridiculed and dismissed for not exhibiting any of the documented signs and bodily features: wide forehead, pointed nose, and so forth. One particularly stubborn claimant with some religious education appeared on the scene when I was in fourth grade. He took himself very seriously, was talked about a lot, and even made the national press. The day he was killed in a bus crash, our teacher said, "another impostor is gone," but didn't encourage further questions on the subject from the class. I knew Lady Saria would be more outspoken on the matter, anyway. So I saved my inquiry for after school.

"How do we know this man was a fake?" I asked Lady Saria that afternoon. "It is quite obvious from the way the man met his death," she replied with no hesitation. "It is written that the real Imam will be murdered by a bearded woman."

What's in a Surname?

"Death to Radjavi!" exclaims the Persian graffiti on the wall of this London Underground station. It is not the first such slogan I've faced since I entered the subway a few minutes ago. The name on the wall coincides with mine, but I am not the target of the threatening message, I know. I also know who it is they wish dead. I just happen to share this very uncommon Iranian surname with the target of the slogan. It is an unsettling experience, nevertheless. And it will occupy my mind at least for the duration of my long subway ride. It is a warm spring afternoon of 1982, and I am on my way to King's College to give a lecture in mathematics. My talk is prepared, but I'd planned to put the finishing touches to it during the ride. This is going to be impossible, I see now. As I try to make myself comfortable in my seat and open my notes, I am distracted, surrounded—besieged, really—by my surname memories, both recent and remote.

The carefully calligraphed political message on the station wall is referring to the leader of a faction in the recent Iranian Revolution—a losing faction. He is the archenemy of the winning side, now in power. It is a curious coincidence that his family and mine—and no other Iranian family, as far as I know—share this last name. Elders of our respective families must have applied for a surname around the same time but in different locations, and with no knowledge of each other's existence.

Nobody in Iran had an officially registered, Western-style last name before the end of World War I. True, there was a notable minority, consisting of current or former aristocratic families, who had "*laghabs*." This meant a title given by, or purchased from, the kings who ruled the country before the Constitutional Revolution of 1906. Such honors, came in very flowery language, usually Arabic, and were always bestowed on male citizens, with the exception of a few favorite Royal wives and concubines. A laghab did serve as a surname, but it wasn't hereditary. No matter how much a man loved his father's title, "Pillar of the Kingdom," for instance, or "Prince of the Scholars," he had to either earn his personal laghab, or pay the Shah of the time for it. After all these years, I can still hear the young men in Ali Khan Close, where I was born and raised as a boy, making fun of an aged neighbor of ours behind his back. The feeble old man, an impoverished aristocrat, strongly preferred to be addressed as "Sentry of the Land." This was the title he had earned in some long-forgotten war waged by a monarch of the preceding dynasty against a disobedient tribe. He wasn't quite satisfied with the shortened version "Mr. Sentry," now his official last name, registered with the Bureau of Vital Statistics. Whenever he signed a letter with "Sentry," he made sure to add in parentheses, "Formerly, Sentry of the Land."

It was a dozen years after the Constitutional Revolution, that the first official identity card in Iran was issued—interestingly, for a female infant. Seven years later, the titles given or sold by the Shahs of yore were all declared illegal by Reza Shah, the founder of the new dynasty, the determined modernizer of Iran. Every household head was now required by law to choose a surname and get an identity card for each member of his family. The titled aristocracy discovered a convenient recipe—the one Mr. Sentry had happily made use of: they tried to stick to an abbreviation of their hard-earned laghab. This clever way of hanging on to remnants of high-class dignity worked so long as there was only one applicant for such a shortening in a given district. Thus if there lived a "Pillar of the Kingdom," a "Pillar of the Army," and a "Pillar of Knowledge" in the same town, the one who applied first got the surname "Pillar." The second applicant would probably go for something like "Pillar's Son." The third applicant, if still insisting on being a Pillar, would have to augment it with a longer word, say, the name of his native town or the first name of his father. Here was a chance, by the way, not just for the titled individuals themselves, but also for the ambitious offspring of a long-deceased "Glory of the Empire," who could reclaim the first word of the laghab. They could then proudly explain the origin of their officially acquired modern family name to the future generations.

Most citizens, of course, didn't have a laghab to work with. The literate among them invented imaginative surnames, borrowing from history and mythology. You could tell from their mere surnames whether they or their fathers, whoever picked the name and officially applied for it, was religious or patriotic, for example. They belonged to the former group if they chose a name from the Holy Scripture; to the latter if they picked a name from the

Persian epic, the *Shahnameh*, Book of Kings. Certain laghab holders actually found it advisable to abandon vestiges of their former laghabs—especially if the laghab referred to a vocation or a duty under the former kings which no longer sounded fashionable or respectable. If your title was "Master of the Interior," everybody knew that this had nothing to do with the newly established position of Ministry of the Interior. It simply meant that you had once been in charge of a former king's large harem—that is, the interior, the inner sanctum, of the royal palace—with hundreds of the Shah's wives, concubines, maids, and eunuchs. A particularly learned and respected citizen of Tabriz during my school years was such a former employee of the Royal Court's Interior. Perhaps he used to have a laghab like "Right Hand of Master of the Interior," but now that the old dynasty was gone, he had acquired an unrelated, short surname. It wasn't just his superior education, I might add, that had earned him his new job as a school principal in the modern educational system. Just as important was his other qualification: he was a eunuch, of course. How else could the bygone king entrust him with the task of managing his harem? And how else could the current, modern Government appease the ultra-conservative guardians of the Faith who, in the absence of eligible female candidates, would rather have no high school for girls at all than put a *man* in charge of such a sensitive institution?

A great number of ordinary surname seekers found easy formulas: they made use of the first name of a deceased father or grandfather; the name of an ancestral village; the trade, or the skill, by which a prominent member of the family was known. They then added a prefix or a suffix, say, a "*zadeh*," meaning "son of" or an "*i*," simply meaning "of." If you were from the town of Salmas, as was my own family, then Salmasi was an easy option. These choices, obviously limited in number, had to be mixed and matched for variety. The illiterate majority tried to get help from friends or neighbors. But, more often than not, they were reduced to accepting readily available assistance from the clerks at the Bureau of Vital Statistics. Judging from family names I would later encounter in school, some of these clerks were either very cruel or almost as illiterate as the applicants themselves. A particularly long and awkward surname of one of my schoolmates could be partially translated as "The Chief *Ghamazan* of Garamalik." The last word is just a village name. The word Ghamazan, however, is less easy to translate. Literally, it means "one who stabs someone or something with a dagger or saber." In the present context, it should be said right away, the stabbing is understood to be done to oneself. It is performed, together with other religious acts of self-flagellation, to commemorate the martyrs of the Faith. These acts take place on certain days of each lunar year. Embarrassed by this distinction, my schoolmate filed an official application with the Bureau of Vital Statistics for a surname change as soon as he finished high school and hoped to go to college and become a teacher of modern literature.

Another way of distinguishing between two families applying for the same desirable surname was to add something like "the second" to a name already spoken for. But less modest applicants blatantly augmented an existing surname with "the original" or even "the first" to make it their own. I vividly remember a sign on the door of a practitioner of astrology and occult medicine. "Soothsayer," read the sign—in my free and very approximate translation. This clever sign announced two things at the same time: a surname *and* a current, not quite legal, profession. In the context understood by the locals, the full name also implied that the home-and-office combination belonged to somebody from a long line of soothsayers. Less than a block away, was an almost identical sign on another door, advertising similar services by a different man. Again the profession was implied by the family name: "Soothsayer the Original."

Some important men seized the opportunity to increase their own family prestige by helping their employees with surname choices: If they chose "Hamid's Son" for their own surname, say, then they graciously recommended "Hamid's Son's Servant " for their head-servant's family.

I HAVE GATHERED, MOSTLY FROM MY MOTHER, that Father had, for several years, resisted bureaucratic pressures to apply for a last name. Forever suspicious of every reform the new Federal Government attempted, Father would cooperate with the agents of change only if it was absolutely necessary. A decade before I was born, it became absolutely necessary to pick an official last name for the family. Not just because the Government imposed a heavy penalty on nameless families in 1925. The more compelling reason was that Father needed an identity card to get a passport required for his travel to Mecca in Arabia—a sacred pilgrimage obligatory for any true believer who could afford it. He wasn't happy; he didn't like "unnecessary government control," whose real and hidden intentions, he was sure, could only be sinister. "Why wasn't a surname necessary before," he kept asking himself and his friends "when I traveled to Karbala, Istanbul, and Tbilisi before the Great War?" But there was no choice now, as his trusted advisor chosen from among the Tabriz clerics reluctantly agreed. (Technically speaking, this cleric was his "source of emulation" in all matters religious.) Most of the clerics had strong reservations about the new order; they were correctly predicting other, even more objectionable, social reforms to follow—like dress codes, minimum female age for marriage, and compulsory modern education. Not just for boys, but also, incredibly, for girls.

By the time Father was resigned to be surnamed, he was approaching sixty. Nearly all his friends and neighbors had already acquired family names. And he wanted to select a surname that was as simple and as unpretentious as possible. So his first choice was, naturally, to use his father's given name and apply for the surname "Razavi." Then something happened which caused the change from "z" to "dj"—a very slight variation both in sound and in script, especially in the local tongue. This is as much as my mother could tell me. Nor could my older brothers shed any further light on the matter. "There must have been too many Razavis in Tabriz by that time," is all they could come up with. And, by the time I got really curious about such things, Father was no longer there for me to ask.

NOW ON MY TRAIN RIDE TO KING'S COLLEGE, having been subjected to such a dramatic reminder of my uncommon surname, I can't stop thinking about my father's choice for a surname. I amuse myself imagining possible circumstances that could have led to this choice. I come up with three different scenarios, one of which just has to coincide with the essential truth, but I'll never know which.

Scenario One: Father arrives at the Bureau of Vital Statistics in Tabriz, dressed in his usual drab old-fashioned robe, the *ghaba*. (In the late 1920s the citizenry hasn't yet been forced to change to Western clothes.) "Would you like a family name, my good man?" the clerk asks him, perhaps hoping to have some fun with another tardy, illiterate applicant from the hills having just arrived in the big city. Father presents him with his beautifully hand-written application forms filled in triplicate as required, all in black ink. "Not another Razavi!" sighs the clerk dismissively, "I am sorry, but this surname has been taken; and so is, in fact, 'Razavi ye Tabrizi', in case you wanted to add a city name." Turning back to the application form and noticing Father's place of birth, Salmas, the clerk comes up with the expected solution: "Shall I make it "Razavi ye Salmasi?" Father, always a fanatic for brevity and economy, and now also anxious to get it over with, thinks for a moment. "No, thank you," he says and asks for the forms back. This makes the clerk wonder about the old man's impertinence. Until Father produces, out of the huge side pocket of his ghaba, an elaborate *qalamdan*—a combination penholder and mobile ink-pot, which also contains his paperknife and ink-wiper as well as a slim pair of scissors. It dawns on the clerk now that Father can write, and he perhaps filled out his own application forms. Father then further confounds him with his own instant solution to the problem: He carefully picks up one of the trimmed reed pens—not trimmed quill you the reader are perhaps familiar with, but trimmed reed, the kind of pen whose use goes back to Biblical times—from his qalamdan. The clerk puts his fountain pen down, drops his condescending attitude, and keeps watching. Father, equipped with his sharp scissors and just enough ink smeared on the tip of the reed pen, proceeds to neatly scratch and modify the application forms: Relying on his knowledge of Arabic, he changes the one letter "z" to another single letter "dj" to make it "Radjavi"—a trivial alteration in the Persian script, as I have already mentioned—and hands it back to the now more deferential clerk. The altered name means "of hope," albeit via a rare and unusual grammatical construction.

Scenario Two: While waiting at the Bureau of Vital Statistics, Father meets another delinquent and reluctant surname seeker. They commiserate about the evil necessity. "What name are you applying for?" the man inquires. "'Razavi,'" says Father. "We are distant cousins, then," the man infers happily, "I am a *Seyyed* also." This is a statement of his privileged position among the faithful: membership in the prestigious class of direct descendants of the Prophet. "But I don't have the honor," says Father, apologetically. This makes the man slightly indignant. There is an unwritten rule of courtesy, he informs Father, by which certain surnames are supposed to be claimed only by Seyyeds. Just like "Alavi" and "Musavi," the man explains, the surname "Razavi" indicates the branch through which the holder of the name has a direct connection to the Holy House of the Prophet. "It would imply," the man tries to enlighten Father further, "that the holder is a descendant of the Eighth Infallible Imam." Father has no such claims—he knows that to qualify for membership, the connection in question has to be through a chain of male ancestors exclusively until it reaches the prophet's daughter and her husband, the First Infallible Imam in the seventh century. Father's mother did happen to be a Seyyed, because her father was. But the entitlement stopped there. The honor could not be inherited from a female. And Father knows this; he is not a seyyed, and he considers it a major sin to pretend. He is embarrassed that he hasn't heard of this new, unwritten rule of courtesy among surname applicants. The surname has to change. Definitely.

(I learned something more in this connection from friends in elementary school. If your mother is a Seyyed, but your father isn't, then it seems that you get partial credit. In such a case you are a Seyyed once a week only: the whole day each Friday. So my father was a Seyyed every Friday, a fact that had an immediate and very logical consequence for me: Given that inheritance from a male parent was total and direct, I was a Friday Seyyed, I decided, with no contribution required from my mother's side. I shouldn't have reported the happy news to Father. "It is an old wives' tale," he said, "your premise is wrong; and so is your conclusion." I didn't tell Father about the rest of my logical conclusions. I was going to run to my nephew next and inform him of *his* small rank in the honour scheme I had just discovered: He is my sister's son, you see, and my sister, I'd figured before I talked to Father, was of course a Friday Seyyed, just like me. But I further deduced from my logical setup that, being a woman, she could transfer only one seventh of her personal honor to her children. Thus my nephew's entitlement would be for only once every 49 days; that is, once every seventh Friday.)

Scenario Three: Father is granted the name "Razavi" as requested, probably because the Vital-Statistics clerk is too lazy to do a thorough check for precedents. Father starts to get uncomfortable when he notices, after a while, just how common his chosen surname is. He gets scared when he contemplates all possible dire consequences of mistaken identity. He still vividly remembers the Salmas massacres, only a decade earlier, in which more than a few of his relatives and acquaintances lost their lives. He remembers a particular relative who would have lived if he hadn't shared a name and a father's name with the real target of the moment in the Great War. He gets worried: what if another Abbasali Razavi, even in a different town, got into trouble with the Government, say, with the Tax Office, and the taxman came after Father by mistake? Who would want more involvement with the Government? Better safe than sorry. Thus he panics and rushes back to the Bureau and applies for a surname change: not "Razavi," not "Razavi e Salmasi," Mr. Clerk, but just plain "Radjavi," please. May I just change one letter in the surname? Thank you.

Whichever way it happened, the name changed. And it remained short and, Father must have hoped, unshared by another family. I too thought for a long time that it was unique. Until, a quarter century after its acquisition, when my brother Kazem, the poet, was shocked to see poems published by another Kazem Radjavi. With the same full name as his. The poetry was "not bad, either," he allowed uncharacteristically, "but not my style." He was worried that his fans, used to the strictly classical form of his own verse would be confused. But this was in peace time, thirty years ago. Now retired and still living in Tehran, while a long and ruinous war is going on with Iraq, my poet brother has had two more memorable experiences brought about by his shared name—in the space of just three years since the Revolution of 1979.

The first occurred soon after the formation of the new theocratic republic. He kept receiving congratulatory phone calls from people he hardly knew: they had just heard on the radio that Kazem Radjavi was appointed the nation's Ambassador to the United Nations Office in Geneva. If the callers were hoping to gain a friend in high places, they were disappointed by the wrong Kazem Radjavi at the other end of the line.

The second, a far more ominous experience, started not too long after the first, and is still continuing to keep my brother on edge: As the Revolution went on, the Ambassador, a brother of the real object of today's graffiti on the London Subway walls, became a target for revolutionary punishment himself. (He will stay on the wanted list of the current regime for eight more years, in fact, until he is assassinated in Switzerland in 1990.) Meanwhile, my brother, the wrong Kazem Radjavi, an entirely apolitical citizen in his old age, has reason to be nervous in his war-torn country. When answering the phone these days, he prudently lengthens his

surname to what that clerk in the Bureau of Vital Statistics
had helpfully suggested to my father so long ago: "Radjavi-ye
Salmasi speaking." He also counsels me to do likewise when
traveling in Iran. "Just to be on the safe side," he whispers.
Wasn't it just a year ago, he asks to refresh my memory, when
rumors spread about Sadegh Khalkhali, the hanging judge
of the Revolution who executed the wrong guy for certain
counter-revolutionary activities? What good was the executioner's attempt at mitigation, offered in reply to a meek
note of protest uttered by a young follower? "No worry if the
executed boy was innocent," the judge was widely reported
to have said, "in which case he is going directly to Paradise,
as you well know." A totally persuasive response to the
young man's reaction—assuming the protester was as true
a believer as the executioner himself seems to have been.

I INTERRUPT MY THOUGHTS of the current war and
revolution in Iran. I take out my lecture notes and try
to bury my painful thoughts in them. No use. When the
train stops at the next station, it is impossible to ignore the
extended list of death wishes calligraphed in Persian. The
additional Iranian surnames mentioned on the wall are
all more common than mine. I wonder if the graffiti is as
jolting to the unsuspecting holders of those surnames as it
was to me. I postpone reviewing my notes and close my eyes.
I succeed in temporarily leaving the present, the immediate
past, the war, the executions, the terror. I take refuge in the
memories of modern surnames again.

I can picture the sad face of a friend and classmate in
ninth grade, obviously perturbed every time our language

teacher tried to pronounce his surname. The name was "Eulmasin," a Turkish word whose literal meaning in my native tongue is "May he not die"—quite an original surname I'd always thought. The first vowel in the name, indicated by "eu," approximates the sound in the French "*bleu.*" The teacher, from a different province of Iran, could only speak Persian. He kept calling my friend "Olmasin," a natural mispronunciation for him, given his language background—the Persian language does not have the sound "eu." Unfortunately for the student, the altered sound gives the word a diametrically opposite meaning in Turkish : "May he not be." The teacher did this consistently and innocently, as any Persian-speaking person would. And every time he did so, we, the students, laughed aloud cruelly, as any group of insensitive boys could. (I was reminded of this mispro-nunciation years later, in the 1960s, when I met an Iranian student in Indiana, a very prim and proper young man, who was once invited to speak to a women's church group. His surname was *Behbehani*. A name the chair of the session did her best to pronounce the way Mr. Behbahani himself did. If you are a native speaker of English, inexperienced in Middle-Eastern languages, try to pronounce the name. Then you won't be surprised at all to hear that the student was, to his great embarrassment, introduced to the group as "Mr. Baby-Honey." His fellow-students teased him by embel-lishing the story. They claimed that the mispronounced introduction had also included his first name, *Abol-ghasem,* which was equally exotic to the American ear: "Ladies, I give you Mr. Apple-Blossom Baby-Honey.")

I don't want to see any more graffiti on the subway station walls. I keep my eyes shut and revisit one last surname memory: I remember the day in tenth grade when I was summoned to the school principal's office. His knotted eyebrows and narrowed lips were definite indications that I'd done something really bad, but I had no clue. "My son," he addressed me in his habitual stern but genuinely fatherly tone, "I must tell you: you should never go to the Culture House. Never, ever!" I was shocked. I hadn't been to the Culture House at all. I'd been curious enough, but afraid to be seen in its immediate vicinity, even. You see, "Culture House" was an abbreviation for "The House of Soviet-Iranian Friendship and Culture." I knew that being seen entering or exiting that building, located in the only public park of Tabriz, would entail serious summonses to my father and me by the Police Department. There the authorities would want to measure the degree of my susceptibility to communist propaganda. I liked to think that I could handle such a situation. But my father couldn't. And I certainly couldn't handle my father. So, I'd stayed away from the Culture House. "Sir," I said to the principal, "I have never set foot in that place." I had to repeat myself several times. And every time he countered by repeating, "But I am not saying that you have, my son; all I am saying is: you shouldn't." His obviously true and flawlessly logical statement was maddening. I wasn't allowed to leave his office that day until I promised never to go to the Culture House. He did call me back to his office a few days later. "It wasn't you, my son," he was happy to report. "It was Radjabi, another student. The similarity of the names must have confused the police who contacted me." This student had indeed been in trouble with the Tabriz police for frequenting the house in question. It seemed to me that the Culture House was situated in that prominent location of our city with the sole purpose of aiding the local police with their anti-communist activities. There must exist, I figured, a reciprocal establishment in the central park of Baku—the large city on the other side of the border, in the Soviet Union—a House of Irano-Soviet Friendship and Culture, to help the soviet police with *their* daily anti-capitalist chores.

THE REMEMBRANCES COME TO AN ABRUPT END at my last subway stop. I arrive at King's College. I have an hour for a final review of my notes. Then I am led to the seminar room in the Mathematics Department to give my lecture. I take a look at the audience, and see many unfamiliar faces. One of them looks particularly unhappy and perhaps unfriendly. Maybe he is just a hard-working graduate student who didn't get much sleep last night. Maybe he didn't want to attend this talk, but his supervisor made him. Not an entirely uncommon sight at a seminar, I know. But then again, under the circumstances, he does look like a fellow-countryman of mine who is perhaps capable of producing those threatening slogans in Persian on the walls of the London Underground. What if he is a literal believer in the slogans? What if he decides the world will be a much more desirable place with one fewer Radjavi? Any Radjavi?

When the chair of the session introduces me, the lecturer, as "Radjavi," I am nervous. I remember my brother

Kazem's advice about our family name. And for a brief moment I consider acting on it: shall I correct the chair—just to be on the safe side? Shall I reintroduce myself as "Radjavi-ye Salmasi"? No, I decide. I will be brave.

As I begin my presentation, I can't help glancing nervously at the young man who has aroused my suspicion. Fortunately, I am able to put him out of my mind as soon as I immerse myself in the safe world of pure mathematics. I become slightly anxious again when he approaches me after the talk. But he is the one who finally puts me at ease. Pointing at one of my statements on the blackboard, he asks me to clarify a technical point: "Does this theorem also hold if the underlying Hilbert space is not assumed to be separable?"

Justice Couldn't Wait

I committed my second, and last, act of vandalism when I was a fully grown man, a supposedly respectable professor at an Iranian university. It had been some twenty years since my first such act, which was described at the time as "uncivilized but just" by my best friend and accomplice in the act. Would he be as agreeable this time around, I wondered, if he were to see what I was just about to do?

It was late in the afternoon of a hot spring day. I'd just left my office in the Arts and Science Building, and was starting my walk home through the university grounds. I was accompanied by Hamid, a junior colleague, a teaching assistant. I took a small coin from my pocket and unabashedly made a long scratch along the passenger side of the fancy new car that belonged to the university president. Hamid looked shocked, but not at all displeased. "He deserves worse," he said. We quickened our pace. It was getting dark; so if the president's personal chauffeur, lounging in the tea-room of the nearby building, keeping an eye on his boss's automobile, could see us through a window, he wouldn't recognize us from behind.

"He is a sycophant," said my young companion, when we had safely left the campus, "he has no business being a university president. He just pretends to be a scholar and an academic. He should have stuck to one of those top cabinet positions in the Shah's Government which he held before he became our president. Doesn't he want to be closer to the monarch he so admires and praises in every speech he delivers?" I knew where Hamid was coming from. The president was not liked much by the angry young members of the university community, most of whom were far to his left on every political issue. It didn't help the president that he had been a radical leftist himself in his youth. Hamid, now a graduate student as well as a teaching assistant, proceeded to recount his own unpleasant experience with the university administration during the previous year, when he had participated in student protests.

Hamid and his friends trusted me with their potentially dangerous expressions of anti-establishment sentiments, although they knew my politically active days were far behind me. They thought this regrettable, of course, but they forgave me and my ilk among the faculty, because we concentrated on our academic jobs, and distanced ourselves from politics of all varieties, local or national. Actually, it worked in my favor that I didn't show preference toward any of the several mutually opposing factions among the student activists. Every "politically aware" student—opposed to the Shah's rule, by definition—belonged to one or the other of two very roughly defined camps: the secular camp and the religious camp. The former included firm believers in Western-style democracy as well as ardent proponents of classless society—anomalous though this must have sounded to outsiders. The latter counted some "religious Marxists" as members, but was dominated by the fast-growing movement that preached a "return-to-self" ideology and loathed what it called "Westoxication."

Hamid, as he had made it clear to me during our frequent student-teacher picnics, decidedly belonged to the secular camp. He had no problem with an occasional beer while heatedly arguing concepts as profound as "historical necessity" and "dictatorship of proletariat" with a member of the religious camp—who would not touch the stuff in the bottle, and would probably interrupt any discussion, no matter how heated, for the purpose of saying their oblig- atory noon or afternoon prayers. I, as one of the older and wiser presences among the picnickers, wasn't expected to take sides, of course. But I found it uplifting to watch these idealistic young people get along so well. The only slightly negative feeling the camps had toward each other was benign pity: how could the other side be so blind to the obvious truths? Constant friendly discussions did, however, lead to an occasional defection, a switch of camps, an adjustment of truths. As I write this over forty-five years later, I wonder if anybody at that time and place could even imagine the state of affairs to come, in a mere six or seven years, when the two camps would become mortal enemies. This would happen in 1979, as soon as their joint efforts contributed to the success of the revolution that overthrew the common enemy, the last Iranian Monarch, King of Kings, Light of the Arians.

My walking companion didn't seem too curious about the reason for my vandalism that day. Was Hamid hoping, perhaps, that I had finally seen the light again and that my youthful revolutionary rage had returned? Was he afraid to ask? Probably. I knew how trivial my motivation would sound to him, but I decided to risk it. I explained myself by pointing to the large, prominently displayed sign that read, "Parking Strictly Prohibited on This Road at all Hours." The president's large car was parked, as if defiantly, right next to the sign, and was actually impeding the normal flow of traffic. "And this isn't the first time either," I further justified my act to Hamid. "And, as you know, no other parking is tolerated at this spot. I wasn't even allowed yesterday to have a cab wait for me at this location just for a couple of minutes while I was grabbing a book from my office. I bet you that the local cop in charge of traffic is tempted to do what I just did, every time he walks by, sees this particular car, and is too scared to ticket it. He knows the dire consequences of treating a powerful man as an ordinary mortal." (If you happen to be reading this account now, dear former president, you may recognize yourself, and may remember the year, the car, and the scratch. You, too, must have assumed at the time, with some degree of self-congratulation, that the scratch was a statement by a rebellious student who disagreed with your political views. Sorry to disappoint you at this late date: it was just a traffic ticket you thought you would never get.)

"Your personal reason doesn't matter that much," my young companion lied graciously. "He deserved it anyway." We'd reached his bus stop now, and it was time to say bye. As I resumed my long walk home, I was unrepentant but preoccupied. Mixed memories of my first "uncivilized but just" act, and the circumstances that had led to it, were now revived. I remembered exactly how Hussen, my friend and partner in crime, had reacted. I remembered how ideologically motivated he and I were as fifteen-year-old high school students. Maybe I should have shared my recollections with Hamid. Surely he would have found the reasons for my first act less trivial, less disappointing than those for the one I had just committed. Perhaps I would tell him sometime. For now I walked home, and I remembered.

HUSSEN AND I, TOGETHER with a few other ninth- and tenth-grade students in the Ferdowsi High School of Tabriz, were members of the editorial board of a magazine called "*The Guide for Youth.*" Our founder and editor-in-chief was Akbar Agha, a twelfth-grader who already thought of himself as a thoroughly dedicated social reformer—and he would stay true to his ideology for the rest of his life, doing time as a political prisoner both before and after the 1979 Revolution. The first issue of The Youth Guide had already been printed, published and, we liked to think, made waves. One of the lead articles of this issue, written by Akbar Agha himself, had fiercely attacked the National Department of Education for "encouraging the forces of reaction and superstition in society, all in the name of promoting religious activities." It was referring, among other things, to the fact that public school facilities had been used for self-flagellatory mourning processions by religious groups in commemoration of the Martyrs of the Faith. Inspired by this article, Hussen and I wanted to write a firsthand account on prevalence of superstition in our society. To appear in a future issue of The Guide for Youth, it would be a "*reportage*"—as the media of the day fashionably called

such accounts, always with the original French pronunci-
ation. The two of us agreed that we should pay a visit to a
"professional" representative of superstition, an advertised
claimant to supernatural powers. We picked a *do`anevis*. The
literal meaning of this all-encompassing term is "prayer-
scriber." But it has always been used more generally to refer
to any person claiming to hold at least a few skills ascribed to
professionals from a long list: psychic, soothsayer, spellcaster,
astrologer, fortune teller, palm reader, sorcerer, medicine
man, and faith healer. We picked a do`anevis who practiced
in the older quarters of the city. We decided that, for best
results, one of us should pay him a visit as a "patient"—
visits by both of us would be neither entirely necessary nor
easily affordable. We tossed a coin and I won the chance to
pose as a young man in hopeless love and in dire need of
professional help.

One afternoon, after school, Hussen and I arrived at the
do`anevis's work place, much like a doctor's office. Instead
of framed medical certificates, however, pictures of mysterious talismans and posters of calligraphed prayers adorned
the walls. There were also framed copies of testimonials by
recognizable clients. And a dignified, bearded, and turbaned
photograph of the do`anevis's father from whom he had
inherited his skills, his job, and his office. There were quite a
few patients in the waiting room. We took our seats, waited,
and tried to be as observant and as attentive to details as
we imagined authors of a soon-to-be-published reportage
ought to be. Seated next to me, for example, I curiously
surveyed a sickly young boy accompanied by his mother.
Across the fairly large waiting room from me, I spotted an

apparently healthy but sad-looking man in his early twenties. His complaint, I guessed, must be similar to the one Hussen and I had cooked up for me to present. When my turn finally came, it was already starting to get dark outside. I figured that the man had seen at least thirty customers that afternoon. I entered the inner office and faced the imposing figure of the tall, handsome, middle-aged man with a long black beard, dressed in the traditional scholar's robe and turban, who discreetly demanded his fee in advance. I was of course prepared for this, and presented him with a crisp five-gran bill, the sum of equal contributions to the cost of this joint adventure by Hussen and myself. "Put it in that glass jar on the table, please," he instructed me with an appropriate show of disdain for the evil necessity of talking about, or dealing with, money. He then inquired about the district of Tabriz I came from, which I decided to answer truthfully. Had he asked for my name, he would get a pen name, of course.

"Let me guess," said the do`anevis with a slight, big-brotherly smile on his lips, "you are in love with a neighbor girl." Love was my planned complaint, true. But why "neighbor," I wondered for a moment. Why was he taking a risk? Couldn't the object of my adulation and cause of my malaise come more conveniently from a richer and more modern part of the city, where the male-female socialization codes were not as strict as my district? But I was able to resolve the puzzle before it could unduly affect my performance. I decided that the risk he took was calculated: One of the three Christian churches of Tabriz happened to be in my neighborhood. This provided an opportunity for me and my neighbor boys to see more girls with exposed faces than we would normally encounter in most of the other old parts of the city. "How did you know?" I now asked the do`anevis, feigning great amazement. He just shook a sympathetic, all-knowing head, ignored my expression of surprise, and went on with the diagnosis.

"And she is acting as if you didn't exist," he asserted, "Right?"

"Yes, right; yes, of course!"

"Not uncommon, not uncommon at all."

"What should I do?" I tried to look as sad and as desperate as my situation required.

"Well, it isn't easy," he said, narrowing his eyes, curling his lips, and gently rocking his head in concentration, then staring at an imaginary point on the high ceiling of the room for a few seconds, then slowly lowering his gaze and closing his eyes. He let a few more seconds pass in pregnant silence. "But a remedy is possible," he then informed me to my apparent delight. Another short pause followed while he kept his eyes shut.

I had expected a few questions about my girl's surroundings, her age, her school, her parents, and her friends. But the do`anevis wasted no more time. Slowly opening his eyes and seeing how anxious I had managed to look, he went right to the point: "I'll have to prepare a special talisman for you. It'll take several days for me to perfect it, of course, but you'll see its positive effect as soon as you start carrying it in an inner pocket of your jacket at all times." As discreetly as I could pretend, I inquired about the cost. "I know, of course," he replied, "that you are just a student. So I won't charge you any fees. You'll pay the cost only. It'll be 10 tumans." This was much steeper than I had anticipated: twenty times his fee for one visit, the amount I had just deposited in his money jar. I silently congratulated myself on a well-played role as lovelorn boy. "I'll have to wait then," I said politely, "until I have saved enough money. Unfortunately, this would take a very long time; I had no idea of the high cost involved." He had clearly foreseen this possibility. "You shouldn't have to wait at all," he assured me calmly and immediately, "since there is an alternative that is almost as effective as the one I first suggested. And it costs much less. It is a special good luck charm. Quite a few people I've helped, many with limited resources, like yourself, have reported one hundred percent efficacy for my carefully crafted charms. And the cost to you is only three tumans." I said, "Sounds good! I'll try to save this amount in the coming weeks and come back." I took perverse pleasure in his disappointed, perfunctory nod when we said goodbye.

My friend and I left the office and took a walk. He wanted to know every detail of my visit to the inner office, which I was more than happy to share. When I mentioned the prohibitive prices of the suggested solutions for my problem, Hussen wasn't taken as far aback as I'd expected. "You know," he said, "if you were well enough dressed for him to take you for a rich boy, he would have offered more exotic methods of finding your way into your beloved's heart." As an example, Hussen mentioned a rich acquaintance of his family, a true sufferer from unrequited love, who was prescribed an outrageously expensive device by a more flamboyant colleague of our do`anevis—whose office was evidently beyond our reach, financially speaking. "Rumors have it," said Hussen, "that the poor rich fellow is now carrying on his person a device enclosing, among other things, a dried portion of the private parts of a she-wolf hunted and slaughtered for the purpose."

Hussen and I made a few notes in preparation for our job as daring journalists, totally convinced that the man I'd just visited was a fraud. It would be a definitive, damning reportage indeed, what Hussen and I were planning to write jointly. It would have to appear in the third issue of The Guide, we agreed. The second issue was full and in the printers' hands already. We had only one regret now: our article would have to be pseudonymous—our elders strongly disapproved of what they called our adult activities.

The second issue of The Guide for Youth was, alas, to be stillborn: When its printing was completed, two police officers appeared in the printing shop one morning and demanded that all copies of the magazine be put in the two large burlap bags they had helpfully brought along. Our editor-in-chief, Akbar Agha, reported the sad news to us in the school yard that afternoon. The bags were being hauled away, he said, when he arrived for a last-minute inspection at the printer's. "Why? Why?" we cried in unison, we the junior members of the editorial board. The Guide, we were all certain, hadn't done anything that a progressive newspaper or magazine wouldn't do. Akbar Agha didn't know the exact reason for the sudden confiscation. The policemen had simply said that they were following orders. That was it.

A few days later, the editors of The Guide were all repri-
manded by the school principal, in official letters sent to
our homes. No doubt under pressure from the Department
of Education, the principal ordered us to put an end to
our "political activities" at once, explaining that what we'd
meddled in was "clearly none of a student's concern." He
also warned us and our parents that any future repetition
of said misdemeanor would result in tougher actions by the
Department of Education. My father and older brother—
only a dozen years older than me, but habitually acting
as a much wiser man, I thought—both highly conser-
vative citizens, were furious when they saw the letter from
the principal. They wondered about my sanity. It helped
my situation a bit that my own contribution to the first
issue of the magazine, quite unlike the one now in preparation, was not even remotely political, but just a harmless
self-help article, translated from a Turkish magazine. What
had caused the ire of the authorities, I tried to explain, was
another article, by somebody else. No matter. My elders
demanded my total obedience to the principal and my
immediate withdrawal from the editorial board of The
Guide. What did I mean anyway, my brother asked rhetorically, when I put to him that Akbar Agha's commentary was
not really political, but social? Couldn't I see the purpose
behind the action taken by the Department of Education?
Wasn't it obvious that this was coordinated with the general
policies of the Central Government to fight communism?
Wasn't it obvious that these official policies included
promoting everything that the religious masses rightly or
wrongly considered an integral part of their faith?

The day after we received the written reprimands, Hussen and I took a long walk together after school. We commiserated, and discussed our future journalistic plans. The Guide for Youth was now defunct. Like any progressive periodical, we agreed, its chances of survival were slim anyway. The reportage on our man the do`anevis, which we had been so enthusiastically working on, was not going to be published and read now. And we had wasted good money too to get to our subject, the charlatan. We were very angry. Angry, not just at the do`anevis, of course, but also at the principal, at the Department of Education, at the police chief, at our elders—all of them. Why couldn't any of them see the truth? My own anger was mostly directed at the do`anevis. And it was definitely not just his fee. I had never forgotten how my beloved grandmother had been treated, before my time, by an older member of our do`anevis's extended family, probably a paternal uncle—their whole clan had long been believed by many to have supernatural powers. Even as a child I was greatly saddened by the story told by my mother. Which I now related to Hussen:

When Grandmother and Mother, together with other women and children of their hometown of Salmas, fled the massacres of World War I, they had been forcefully separated from the male members of the family on their long walk toward Tabriz, the big city, where they now resided. Mother's older brother, around twenty years old at the time, was never to be heard of again. Grandmother, in her desperation to learn anything about her lost son, consulted the old do`anevis, who prescribed, among other things, an exhausting forty-day regimen. Every day she was to fast dawn to dusk; no food, no water—and this all outside the regular fasting month of Ramazan. And every morning she was to say especially long prayers (sold to her by the psychic himself, of course). She was then to get out of her house, before sunrise, and sweep her side of the street clean. Every day, for forty days. On the fortieth day, her do`anevis promised, she would have a vision: her revered Hidden Imam, the Twelfth Infallible one would appear to her in person after the fortieth morning's street-sweeping. She should then ask him about the fate of her son.

She did all of this dutifully. And she painstakingly kept her husband, my grandfather, in the dark—he was not a believer in induced apparitions. My mother, in her early teens at the time, who was not yet ready to accept the permanent absence of her brother, had also invested some faith in the do`anevis's methods. So she was as disappointed as Grandmother was when no holy vision was observed on that last day of street sweeping. Informed by Grandmother of his method's failure, the do`anevis assumed a puzzled look. He asked her if she sighted anybody at all in that early morning after she'd done the sweeping. Yes, said Grandmother, she had seen an elderly cleric in robe and turban walk by with a bundle of clothes under his arm. And she'd naturally assumed that he was going to the public bath house. (A common sight in the early hours of the day: men always went to the public bath house before work, and before the bath house started to cater exclusively to women and children an hour or so after sunrise.) "Well, did you, or didn't you, put your question to him?" the do`anevis demanded to know. She hadn't, of course. She had seen other men, including clerics hurrying to the bath house practically every morning during the long regimen. But the psychic was adamant. He reminded her sternly, for future reference, that a saint could appear in any respectable guise he himself preferred. But Grandmother was in no shape, physically or mentally, to repeat the strenuous 40-day experiment.

"LET US TAKE A BREAK FROM OUR LONG WALK," said a saddened Hussen after hearing my story. "This would have made a nice addition to our reportage, but … ," he sighed and stopped. We went to an old-fashioned snack shop, and ordered two hot *lablabis*. This was the favorite winter substitute for ice cream—ice cream was strictly a summer delicacy for most citizens of Tabriz in 1950. A lablabi was a whole sweet beet, either red or golden, slowly steam-cooked to perfection in a special clay oven. My friend and I made the observation that the cost of this hot lablabi, fresh from the oven, was a fifth of the fee we'd recently spent on our psychic's fee. What a waste! If only our exposé had been allowed to appear in print! We felt helpless. There was nothing we could do now, it seemed, if the Department of Education, so ridiculously named, was determined to keep us from truly educating the public. Things looked bleak indeed. But, before we finished our hot lablabis, we had an impromptu plan of action. Immediate action.

It was late afternoon by the time we left the snack shop. We went directly to our do`anevis's office. When we arrived, there was only one elderly patient in the waiting room. We waited until the clients inside the examination room left and the last patient went in. Then we attacked the walls of the waiting room. Before the office servant came in for the daily cleaning, we had managed to tear a couple of talisman posters into pieces, break at least one framed testimonial, and run away in an excited mix of fear and glee.

Thus went my first act of vandalism, a joint effort with Hussen. It was six years after Grandmother's death. I justified my act to myself as I pictured her kindly, wrinkled face— vivid in my mind not just then, but even now as I write this, sixty-five years later. I imagined how helpless she must have felt when, unbeknownst to her disapproving husband, she visited a reigning do`anevis of Tabriz for guidance. Hussen and I felt satisfied. "It was uncivilized but just," he said more than once. "Uncivilized but just," I echoed each time he said it. The do`anevis was definitely a charlatan, we reconfirmed each other's conviction; even if his distant ancestors in the same business hadn't been. Those other members of his family, who belonged to my grandmother's generation, had possibly believed in their clan's God-given supernatural powers. After all, they didn't have the advantage of living right in the middle of the enlightened twentieth century. There was no excuse for the clan now, Hussen and I agreed whole-heartedly. There was certainly no excuse for the Department of Education to interfere with our struggle against superstition.

THE OPPORTUNITY TO RELATE the story of my first act of vandalism to Hamid, the sole witness to my second act, didn't arise for several years. When I came back from a longish stay in Canada and revisited my old university, I found the student activists in a decidedly more serious, in fact quite belligerent, mood. More defections and switches had taken place between the two main camps, and also among the subcamps of either camp. Definite, hostile lines were beginning to be drawn, separating tiny groups from each other. The religious camp had evidently started to gain ground already. Several of Hamid's female friends and fellow-campers, erstwhile secular feminists, were now covering their hair, not just in public, but even when they joined us for lunch at the university cafeteria. Some had converted permanently, they said. And some said they were doing it to show "solidarity" with their religious sisters. A poet friend of Hamid's had quit drinking beer altogether and was said to have burned all his "useless, hedonistic, Western-style" songs. I wondered about Hamid himself. Had he also switched sympathies perhaps? Should I try to find out?

When Hamid and I met for tea one afternoon, just the two of us, he was as correct and polite as ever, but looked a little distracted. I reminded him of our secret, the incident of the illegally parked presidential automobile. He smiled. I was encouraged. "You know," I started, "I had committed another act of vandalism long before the one you witnessed." He was interested. But he became visibly uncomfortable as soon as I mentioned that it was about the youthful stand taken by my comrades and me in opposition to superstition in the name of religion. The juxtaposition of the words "superstition" and "religion" had done it: I could tell right away that he was looking for an excuse for an immediate interruption. I decided to postpone the narration indefinitely when he civilly but firmly stated his current "position on spiritual matters," as he put it.

In an admirable attempt to spare me the embarrassment of recounting my story and facing his dutiful harsh reaction, he said, "It has now become well known that the previous generation"—this evidently included me—"was misguided by its infatuation with the West. Western Imperialism has poisoned our culture by our own hands. It has seduced us into denying our own spiritual values. Of course, it always starts with taking the so-called scientific approach and denying the value of certain rituals which, at first sight, seem primitive, irrational, or even superstitious. But before we know it, our souls are in a totally materialistic hell."

Ouch.

One Picture's Preposterous Power

"Alright, you can eat your sandwiches behind that curtain," said Mashdali the shopkeeper. He was directing me and my friend Habib to his little storage room. "But please be quiet!" he cautioned us, "And don't come out until I tell you the coast is clear." What he was about to do had just been declared illegal by His Majesty's Government. If caught, he would be fined heavily for feeding able-bodied young men in daytime during the "Blessed Month"—the fasting month of Ramazan. Mashdali was a religious man himself, very attentive to his devotional duties, saying all his daily prayers on time and fasting every long day of the Blessed Month. This meant, among other things, eating nothing and drinking nothing, not even water, until after sunset. But Mashdali graciously accepted the medical exemption claims by Habib and me. In fact, he had trusted us enough to feel no guilt in feeding us during the previous year's fasting season, when his act was still legal.

Mashdali was as surprised as my friend and I were by His Majesty's abrupt change of heart this year. Or was it an upsurge in the monarch's religious devotion? The Revolution of 1979, which would bring severe punishments for any public defiance of sacred rules of the Faith, was still almost a quarter century ahead of us. As long as recent generations of students remembered, it had always been possible until the fasting month of this year of 1955, at least in the vicinity of the University campus, to have lunch in restaurants and cafes—so long as you ate indoors to be respectful of the observant public's sensibilities. It was tacitly assumed by the operators of these establishments that the lunch-time clients in Ramazan either belonged to a minority faith group or were otherwise exempt for justifiable reasons, including health and travel. No questions asked, every benefit of the doubt given.

But it was suddenly different this year. "I am very sorry for the inconvenience," said Mashdali sincerely, "but what can I do if I am not rich enough to own a hotel?" He was referring to a clause in the police order he had just received, which forbade restaurants and coffee shops from opening their doors before sunset during the Blessed Month. The order made an exception for hotels, where the clients were automatically assumed to be travelers away from home, and thus permitted by the rules of the Faith to have regular meals. I wondered aloud how Mashdali's shop was allowed to stay open during the day. "Mine is technically a grocery store, not a restaurant," he said, "so I can stay open unless they catch somebody eating here before dark." Habib and I didn't want to cause any trouble for the man, and we promised to be very quiet behind the curtain. "We can't waste time going home for lunch on weekdays," Habib explained. "So let us agree on an excuse, in case somebody accidentally catches us eating." Mashdali thought for a moment, swore at his bad luck again for being too poor to open a hotel, apologized to the Almighty for swearing, expressing hope that his ugly words hadn't spoiled his fast irreparably, and said, "I'll tell them that you are my family friends, and that I know you have doctors' orders. God knows all I am doing is just stretching the truth a bit." This family touch might work, it was agreed, especially because we all had the same mother tongue of Azeri Turkish. "Or, you can say that we are traveling," Habib offered, "and we have just come back from a visit to our hometown." But Mashdali didn't want to lie. Certainly not while fasting.

Habib and I finished our lunch discreetly, behind the closed curtain, and waited there as instructed. When signaled by Mashdali, we came out, paid him, thanked him, and started our walk back to the University. "Traveling is always a good excuse," Habib observed. "If we had a car, for example, there would be no problem at all: we would just have to drive out of town to eat freely, anytime we wanted." He was right. We knew that if you traveled far enough from home, you were allowed to break your fast for the day. "Far enough" was not a loose term: It had been strictly defined by the Fathers of the Faith many centuries ago: it meant a locality where it was no longer possible to hear the prayer calls from the minarets of your hometown. This was common knowledge. We were also aware of a surprisingly permissive ruling by the custodians of the Faith: It seemed to allow you, albeit reluctantly, to plan a trip even with the explicit purpose of avoiding the obligatory fast. This codicil to the sacred rules was particularly convenient to minimalist followers of the Faith when Ramazan happened to fall on hot summer days of the year. (The beginning and end of the Blessed Month, like all religious occasions, have always been precisely determined by the phases of the Moon. And the lunar year has approximately 354 days. So if you have a wintry Blessed Month this year, you'll have a summery one in about 16 years. And vice versa.) Those easy-going members of the Flock who could afford it, simply organized out-of-town picnics on nice, hot days of the fasting month in order to escape their sacred duty without penalty. They knew of course that they owed the Almighty so many full days of fasting in compensation, a debt they could easily and happily pay back in six months' time. On conveniently short winter days.

"There are other ways to get travel exemption," I said to Habib, "and you don't even have to own a car if you are resourceful. Take my mother's cousin Jafar from my ancestral hometown of Salmas, for example. He used to visit my family often—he had business associates in Tabriz. I remember him arriving in Tabriz by bus and then taking a horse-driven cab directly to my house, often entirely unannounced. He was a jovial, sociable, and generous man, and always brought substantial gifts for my parents and me, but his religiosity was rather dubious. His wife had confided in my mother that Cousin Jafar occasionally drank forbidden beverages with friends, and frequently forgot to say his daily prayers—except during the Blessed Month of fasting, when he refrained from drinking altogether, he fasted when not traveling, and he was punctual with his daily prayers. However, when his business trips happened to take him to my household in Tabriz during Ramazan, Cousin Jafar expected and received almost full hospitality, day or night. My mother never neglected to prepare a special, 'guest-worthy' lunch for him, while she herself was fasting conscientiously. To be fair to his memory, I should say that Cousin Jafar never failed to express his deep regret for the unfortunate coincidence of his absolutely necessary business trip with this holy occasion. To prove the point, he got up early every morning with the adult members of the family—who had to have their last meal of the day before dawn, in preparation for the long day's fast—and performed his religious ablutions before saying the morning prayers. He also insisted that this big pre-dawn meal, which he shared with the hosting family, would do for breakfast, and that he would only trouble mother for the mid-day meal. It was unthinkable, of course, for him as well as for my folks, that he should stay in a hotel while in Tabriz, away from his hometown."

"Yes, I have relatives like that too," said Habib, "relatives who live out of town and usually remember to pay my family a visit in the fasting month. They have discovered that we generally eat better and fancier meals during this month—as a partial reward, I guess, for our dutiful observance of sacred rules." He was right about better food: My own mother's tastiest dishes, normally served only on weekends, were now enjoyed by the family every day, before dawn, even with no houseguests present to justify the extra expense.

As we walked toward the University, Habib and I turned back to the burning question of the month, the holier-than-thou attitude assumed by the enforcers of law and order. "Everybody must be wondering," said Habib in his usually cheerful but cynical tone, "Why the change? And why now? Surely nobody is prepared to believe that His Majesty has witnessed apparitions to render him more religious all of a sudden. Or is it to fight communism again?" He was referring to certain government policies which, almost a decade back, had temporarily allowed religious zealots free rein in the name of fighting godless Bolsheviks. "But how can it be?" I asked, "Haven't the Shah's men been claiming that communism no longer posed a national threat after the 1953 coup, which resulted in a total political cleansing?" We agreed that we were clueless, and that we would probably have to wait a long time for a satisfactory answer.

THIS POLICY CHANGE AGAINST DAYTIME EATING wasn't the only surprise in the Blessed Month, as it turned out. A well-known cleric, a celebrity in fact, the formidable M.T. Falsafi, began to deliver fierce public sermons warning the faithful citizenry about "the members of the wayward *Baha'i* sect, who are much worse than heretics, much worse than materialists, and, yes, much worse than communists." We knew that clerics were, as a rule, opposed to this minority sect, but its members had usually been protected by the Government against open and public harassment— certainly in the last few decades, at least. We were baffled by the well-known preacher's tirades broadcast on the state radio, right after the prime-time news hour, every day of the month. The timing was of course deliberate: it guaranteed the speaker a maximal audience of fasting believers, caught in the devotional fervor that always came with the Blessed Month.

"Listen to me, you the faithful!" Falsafi admonished his large radio audience one weekend afternoon, when Habib and I were tuned in to him together, "You parents of impressionable young boys! Listen to me carefully! Have you ever asked yourselves where your teenage sons are spending their after-school hours? I'll tell you where: it has come to my attention that quite a number of them are going to the Baha'i Centre, where they are received with open arms and treated with delicious snacks and soda. And do you know who is serving the snacks and soda? I'll tell you who: young, attractive Baha'i girls with no head-covers! Yes, these girls not only serve your innocent adolescents snacks and lemonade; they also play ping-pong with them! Yes, you probably didn't know this, did you?" A strong believer in the art of persuasion by repetition, Falsafi went on: "And what do you think happens to an impressionable young, past-puberty boy, when he goes to the Baha'i Centre, is served sweet snacks and lemonade by an attractive Baha'i girl with no head-cover, who also invites the boy to a game of ping-pong—right there, under this supposedly sacred dome, in this so-called temple? What else? What else? He eats the snacks, he drinks the lemonade, and he plays ping-pong with a hijabless girl, and—it is not surprising at all, is it?—he is naturally attracted to this false religion. The next step for these infidels is, of course, to make their poisonous, deceitful literature available to your boy. And before you know it, you have a Baha'i in the family. Do you hear me? A Baha'i in your own family! Yes, parents, wake up! Hear me well! Do something! If and when it is too late, God forbid, don't you go around saying that I didn't warn you! I am warning you now!" Yes, he did speak exactly like this. I can still hear him say these words. It is still in my head after more than sixty years.

Falsafi's sermons gave me an excuse to tease Habib about Haida, the Baha'i girl he'd had his first crush on. Haida was his neighbor when she and Habib were both in high school a few years back, in our home city of Tabriz. "So now I know why you liked Haida so much," I said. "She must have served you biscuits and lemonade in the Baha'i temple and played ping-pong with you." I had no idea just how sore a point this was with Habib. "I wish!" he said with a deep sigh. His habitually cheerful voice was suddenly gone. "I never got a chance to say hello to her, even. Her family and mine, true believers, each in their own faith, avoided each other as much as it was possible for neighbors to do so. If our fathers were forced by circumstance to exchange greetings in the street, they used words different from their normal salutations, those reserved for the truly faithful among their own people. The women, it seemed, could get along a little better than the men did. Our mothers had no problem exchanging hellos in their simple everyday language. They even politely inquired about each other's health. Inviting a Baha'i home, however, was of course an entirely different matter. For one thing, anything touched by a wet hand of such a visitor to my household, as well as any teacups, plates, and cutlery used by the guest, would have to be given a ritual washing and cleansing. This would be an extremely difficult task if a large item like a carpet or a piece of heavy furniture was so contaminated by the accidental spilling of tea from a cup that had touched the guest's lips." I asked Habib if Haida ever knew about his feelings towards her. "No, never!" Habib reminisced, "I was totally in love with Haida, but all I could manage was to catch a glimpse of her beautiful face on the way to or from school every weekday. Until I left Tabriz for college. Then she got married, to a young man of her own faith, of course. No biscuits and soda, no ping-pong, and no attempts at any conversion. Sorry to disappoint you." I had never seen Habib so serious before. Had this bitter experience played a role, I wondered, in forming his present cynical attitude toward almost everything in Iranian society—religion, politics, and education?

As the Blessed month progressed, the famous preacher kept enlightening his flock about the wayward sect. As if encouraged by his cheering audiences, he and his colleagues expanded on an incredible theory of his—already more than hinted at by him—of a link between the communists and the Bahai' sect. "These guys are really good!" Habib mused when he arrived at school one morning. He had just read a booklet put out by another, like-minded, preacher. "This one sounds so convinced; I am sure he believes his own fabrications. He is telling us about a 'first-hand' experience of his. It seems that a repentant communist, a former member of the banned Tudeh Party, has disclosed a surprising fact to him: A large group of the informant's ex-comrades were apparently ordered by the now-underground communist party to join the Baha'i circles and use this 'religious mask' to propagate their own unholy ideas." Remarkable, indeed. For a moment Habib and I wondered if His Majesty himself was also suspecting a link between Marxism and Bahai'sm. "Can't be," said Habib after a brief reflection, "nobody in their right mind can possibly imagine such a link." I caught the opportunity to tease him again, perhaps too cruelly: "Don't be so sure, Habib. How do we know Haida's folks were not masked communists themselves? Think of it: If they were, you missed your golden chance with Haida. I am sure masked communists would have no objections to their daughters' consorting with a fellow-traveler like you. After all, you were yourself called to the police station more than once for alleged left-wing sympathies, even before the big military coup of 1953, even while we were still in high school. Remember?" Habib wasn't amused.

MEANWHILE, THE SERMONS WERE GETTING more and more outrageous. Falsafi was talking of how little time there might be left before the Baha'i infidels took over the country. He was now very close to preaching actual violence against the sect. The puzzle was getting more and more complex: Almost everybody knew that the great preacher wouldn't dare voice even a fraction of his opinions, much less his thinly disguised call for violence, without His Majesty's explicit approval. Still, nobody we knew could come up with a plausible explanation. The provocation got starker by the day. Yet the officially sanctioned cleric kept feigning an anti-violence stance.

"O' the faithful, control your wrath against these infidels, these traitors!" went the exaggerated, mock sermon given by my 13-year-old nephew in flawless imitation of Falsafi's thunderous voice and cutting rhetoric." Yes, while you are fasting, praying, and trying hard to be more obedient servants to the Almighty, these traitors keep saying false prayers and visiting their fake shrines. They fast only 19 days a year instead of a full month, and always in the last part of winter, when the days are shorter and cooler.

I know exactly how you feel, O' the faithful! I know. You want to do something before it is too late. You want to put an end to the devious activities of this blasphemous sect. I know; believe me, I do! But do not, I repeat, do not, under any circumstances, plan to gather together around the Great Mosque at the Bazaar tomorrow morning at 9:30, armed with heavy pickaxes, and—do not, I repeat, do not—march together toward the Baha'i Centre near Yusofabad Square and destroy the temple for good. No, no, never, O' the faithful!" Of course my nephew the young comedian had the benefit of hindsight: He was doing the imitation the day *after* the destruction of the temple, which had actually taken place in broad daylight.

The wrecking operations were, according to the official reports, initiated spontaneously by the faithful adherents to the spirit, if not the letter, of Falsafi's sermons. But the pickaxe-carrying mob of believers was led by a well-known army general, Chief of Staff of the Imperial Army, no less. The mob succeeded in bringing down the huge dome of the Baha'i Centre with no help from any fancy explosives or wrecking balls. News items in the daily papers, the day after the incident, included photographs of the general himself proudly using his hand tools. Nobody was reported to be bodily harmed on that day of pickaxes. But a few days later several Baha'is were killed and some of the sect's provincial centers looted by other spontaneously organized mobs of zealots.

By the end of that holy fasting month, the officially approved harsh punishment for the religious minority— whatever reason had necessitated its initiation—was apparently deemed sufficient for the time being, and we would no longer hear of further related violence for a long while. Of course, we weren't surprised when Pepsi Cola was boycotted by the faithful followers of edicts from some major clerics, because the newly opened Pepsi Cola franchise in Iran was owned by a well-known Baha'i entrepreneur. Not every religious leader was in agreement with this edict, it should be said. In my own religious family, for example, the new, widely advertised, fancy and pricy drink was sometimes served to important guests. I still remember the occasion on which my naughty young nephew was able to appropriate a full, freshly poured glass of bubbly Pepsi as soon as the sought-after drink was served to a religious visitor by my mother. All he had to do, when Mother had temporarily stepped out of the guest room, was to whisper a warning to the guest that the particular major cleric whose instructions she followed (that is, the guest's "source of emulation") had just issued an edict, a *fatwa*, against Pepsi.

OVER 20 YEARS HAD PASSED since our college days, since that unforgettable month of fasting. Habib and I were having dinner at a restaurant in Tehran. My friend, the cheerful cynic, had been growing even more cynical by the year. He, a civil engineer now, and I, a mathematician, worked in different cities of Iran, and had different circles of friends and colleagues, but our paths would cross in the capital city almost every summer. We'd kept in touch during all those years, and this dinner was fondly planned and looked forward to, as always. "I have something interesting to show you," Habib said as he arrived, smiling mischievously, "but let us have dinner first." I was used to his little games of suspense, so I pretended to ignore his remark while we ate. Memories of university days resurfaced, as they did every time we met. Habib mentioned the illegally, if not impiously, consumed sandwiches again. The rules had changed since then. They were more than relaxed now: Many restaurants now served sandwiches on the fasting days of the Blessed Month. Some even served beer, depending on the degree of the restaurant owner's own observance. So, His Majesty was either less pious now, we joked very quietly, or less afraid of the men of cloth. Definitely the latter, we decided. Hadn't the Shah referred to some religious leaders as "the forces of black reaction" in the recent speeches he gave? Hadn't he stuck to his guns with his own "White Revolution," in defiance of most of the clergy, who were opposed to his pronouncements about land reform and women's right to vote? Hadn't he even sent to exile those clerics who had opposed him openly? (Knowing how the monarch had greatly simplified election procedures by practically handpicking our representatives for us, not many citizens took him seriously about his parliamentary reforms. One underground paper had a cartoon depicting a man pleading to the Shah: "Now that you have given my wife the right to vote, I am reminded of the voting right I used to have myself. May I also have it back?"

There was no way at the time for Habib and me to know how drastically everything would change within a mere few years, and how the men of cloth would finally have their say again—this time with a vengeance. For now, His Majesty seemed to be in full control. "Okay," said Habib, "it is established that the Shah no longer needs the support of the clergy in his campaigns against the Red Menace, and he doesn't even care what the religious leaders think of the royal reforms. But what was it that changed so suddenly in 1955, when he had already declared victory over the communist enemies of the nation?" I could sense it: Habib was clearly building up to something. "And His Majesty was certainly not threatened by the Baha'i community in any way whatsoever. Right?" Making sure that I was all ears, he went on. "So, why did he have to allow our great preacher to agitate against this religious sect at that particular time? And why did he let his cops loose against daytime fast-breakers? Surely, our stealthy noon-time sandwiches at Mashdali's little grocery shop weren't His Majesty's prime targets."

"Yes, this has been our big unsolved puzzle for years," I agreed. Habib gave me a satisfied smile. "No more!" he announced triumphantly. "I have the solution to the puzzle now!" "It is right here, in my breast pocket!" He gave me a familiar stern look that said, "Choose to disbelieve me at your peril." Then he produced a faded black-and-white print of a photograph, cut out of an old underground, left-wing publication: a picture of the King together with his former queen Soraya in a scanty two-piece swimsuit, apparently taken clandestinely at some private beach party in Florida, not long before that eventful fasting month of 1955. I was all ears now.

"It is simple!" Habib proceeded to explain: "Blackmail, my friend, simple blackmail! Once the activist clergy got hold of the original of this very photograph, they saw it as a potentially powerful weapon. They knew how repugnant the picture would be, if released, to their faithful followers' sense of propriety and decency. So the weapon was put to use: If His Majesty impeded their religious duties, including their anti-Baha'i sermons during the approaching Blessed Month, then they weren't sure at all if they *could* prevent the imminent wide distribution of the offensive picture."

Fear of Reading

"I wouldn't read it," said Father dismissively. He had only glanced quickly at the preface of the book I'd brought home to read. I couldn't believe my ears. I had expected loud approval when I showed him the book. It was written by a man of cloth and published as a "definitive rebuttal to Ahmad Kasravi's heretical monograph." Father and I were both aware that Kasravi, although a firm believer in God himself, had questioned every tenet of the faith followed by the majority of the nation. We knew that his unorthodox views were considered by every cleric in the country to be detrimental to young minds, including mine. Hadn't Kasravi lost his life, just three years back, because of those blasphemous utterances of his about our revered Imams and martyrs? Wasn't the threat posed by his pen, even after he was physically eliminated by dutiful believers, too serious to be ignored by the faithful?

"But I am told that this book is very good," I managed to protest meekly, "and that it definitively refutes everything Kasravi ever said in his sacrilegious writings." Father's response was even more baffling than his initial reaction: "Don't read it," he said emphatically, "because if you do, you'll want to read Kasravi himself!" The final conclusion, which he didn't have to state explicitly, was clear: I would likely lose my faith as a result of reading Kasravi.

Father didn't know that together with Habib and Hussen, my current classmates in Junior high school, I had already read a few of Kasravi's books. We all felt guilty, especially Habib and I—the two of us came from more conservatively religious families than Hussen's. We wished we hadn't exposed our minds to these writings. We considered it our pressing religious duty to search for a solid counterargument, an antidote. The book I had just presented to Father came from the same store that also sold Kasravi's unorthodox books. Old Amizrahim, a beloved father figure to my friends and me, ran the store with the help of his two sons. His store was our main source of books not found in the school library, or in the public "reading-house," where you were allowed to read the books, but couldn't take them home.

Habib had two advantages over Hussen and me: One was his family's considerable wealth, hence his generous weekly allowance. And the other, perhaps even more important, was his elders' total illiteracy. So he could buy any book he liked, *and* read it in plain sight of his family members. By the time he was 14, he had amassed a small library in his own spacious room which contained, in addition to many regular volumes, quite a few forbidden items. Among them were some by well-known Marxists and some by Kasravi and other rationalist reformers.

Hussen and I had only one advantage over Habib: our relative anonymity. Because of his father's prominent position in the Bazaar, Habib was too well known. Too easily recognizable by the tradesmen, who referred to him defer-entially as "Mr. Haj Ghulam's heir." This made him reluctant to be sighted at certain locations, including our favorite bookstore whose proprietor had, together with his sons, participated in recent antiwar demonstrations organized by communists. Amizrahim himself was not a communist or an atheist. He was actually a deeply religious man. But, unlike our parents, he had no objections to reading books that were critical of our faith, those certain to plant seeds of doubt in our impressionable minds. On the contrary, he encouraged the activity. "True faith comes after profound doubt," he had said more than once, and we could tell that he was speaking from personal experience. His attitude enabled me and my friends, even without fully understanding his dictum about doubt and faith, to read every doubt-spreading book, albeit with a modicum of guilt and fear. So it happened quite often that we would take Habib's cash, supplement it with our own meagre contributions and head for Amizrahim's store. "You didn't buy it from me," I remember the old man saying, whenever he sold us a recently acquired, used copy of a banned or "semi-banned" book that we'd been asking for. (The latter designation was, in those days of relatively free press in Iran, used for the legally printed matter that was illegally banned by the *local* authorities.)

So, there was no way around it: now this large, hard-to-hide volume—written by a clergyman, no less—too had to be read secretly, just like the monograph it was out to refute. This book by an author in full agreement with Father's worldview, written in defence of Father's sacred beliefs and mine, was judged by him to be unfit to read. Secret reading I could manage safely, since Mother couldn't read, and Father wasn't home during the day. But it was the puzzle of his new prohibition that wouldn't leave my mind alone. So what books, if any, would Father now approve of, other than the compulsory school texts?

I KEPT WONDERING. Was Father trying to shield me from a kind of doubt he himself had experienced when he was young? Had he decided at one point that he had done enough unnecessary reading for himself? I didn't dare ask, of course, and the puzzle would bother me for a long time to come. For now I distracted myself by reviewing my own reading history. How limited my reading material had been, only a few years back, during the early school days! It dawned on me now that Father owned so very few religious books himself. Why hadn't I noticed this before, given his knowledge and his strict observance of the rules of the Faith? Surely, he should have saved some textbooks from his own youth, when he started as a serious student of theology? His book collection, in fact, contained only two books that could be called religious in the technical and strict sense of the word—not counting, I mean, the volumes of prose and verse which contained, among other things, fables about, and quotations from, old prophets and saints. One of the two books, a copy of which could be found in every godly household in my neighborhood, sometimes as the only book in the house, was of course the Holy Quran in its original language, Arabic. The other, in Persian, was a sort of handbook for the faithful, written by a scholar of very high rank, usually a living one, that dealt with frequently asked religious questions. It was about everything in our everyday life: daily ablutions and devotions, compulsory prayers, recommended prayers, fasting, pilgrimage, commerce, almsgiving, marriage, divorce, and permissible varieties of sex.

More than a dozen different versions and editions of this book of answers had always been in circulation, each written by a trusted and esteemed scholar. Unless you were a qualified scholar of the Faith yourself, you had to choose a prominent cleric whose edicts, *fatwas,* you strictly obeyed. This cleric would be the so-called "source of emulation" for you and your family. My father, a self-confessed non-scholar after abandoning his youthful clerical ambitions, was no exception. It so happened that his source of emulation had been dead for a couple of years now, but Father was still using the dead scholar's book as a reference for the time being. This temporary measure—the precise technical term for it was "staying with the dead one"—was allowed if you were in the process of searching for a new living source of emulation and hadn't yet succeeded in finding one. Father was definitely picky about the matter. "He is too wealthy for a man of God," he would say when the name of a living candidate was put forward by a friend. Or, "He enjoys being a prayer leader too much." Father's search for a living source of emulation would turn out to be never-ending, by the way. He would actually stay with his chosen "dead one" for the rest of his own life.

I had a special interest in this family answer book. Meant for the man in the street, it was written in simple Persian. So I'd had no trouble reading it even when I was in second or third grade. To be sure, there were certain passages in it that didn't yet make sense to me. I would have to wait a few years, for instance, to understand the questions and answers about different types of marriage, acceptable varieties of sexual acts, and what should precede or follow each of those acts. But most of the contents were quite accessible. I got interested in the questions dealing with the daily prayers—I suppose because I had just perfected my prayer performance under Father's tutelage. This was in preparation for the day the prayers would become obligatory for me in three or four years' time, as soon as I reached the well-defined stage of puberty for boys. I remember how well I had memorized the technical answers to the many so-called "uncertainty" questions. The questions about our prayers that could come up in daily practice. Let us say you were performing the obligatory noon prayer, which consisted of four almost-identical units. And let us say that just as you thought you'd finished the third unit and were ready to start the fourth, you suddenly became uncertain: You were no longer sure whether what you had just gone through was the second or the third unit. What should you do? Well, starting the prayer all over again was not recommended, and there was an efficient solution prescribed for this problem, and for every conceivable problem of this sort. And the solutions were not hard to memorize for me. I have a clear memory—even as I write this account after almost seventy years—of this particular example of uncertainty, because of a very satisfying encounter I had with my old neighbor, Lady Saria the Pious.

"Is your father home?" Lady Saria inquired urgently, when I answered the door one morning. I had just finished my breakfast and was heading to school. "No ma'am, he just left for the bazaar," I informed her, "but I'll see him after school today, if you have a message for him." It turned out that she had to consult Father on a religious matter, as she'd done frequently. (She happened to have the same source of emulation as my family, but could not read the answer book herself.) And, for some reason, she didn't want to wait. So now that my father wasn't home, she had to take a longer walk, to the home of Amirza Hasan, the preacher. She started to leave, hoping to catch the man at home. "I may know the answer, ma'am," I said timidly, to Lady Saria's utter shock, it turned out. "This is not kid-stuff, Heydar," she admonished me sternly. "Don't be impertinent!" Her words were very insulting to me, the almost-11-year-old boy due to get an elementary school diploma in less than a year. But I managed to keep my cool. "Why don't you just ask me this once, please?" I reasoned with her as politely as I could, but confidently. "And later you can confirm my answer with Father or with Amirza Hasan if you wish." She reluctantly posed her problem: the case of uncertainty between the second and third units of the daily noon prayer. I knew the remedy by heart, from Father's book of answers.

"You should assume that you've done the third unit," I said to Lady Saria with as much authority as I could muster. I pictured myself as Amirza Hasan the preacher answering a similar question posed by a member of his flock, and went on: "And continue your prayer with this assumption. But when you are done, you must add a one-unit *ehtiat* prayer"—I used the correct technical term which meant "to act cautiously, to be on the safe side." Wow! I had done it; I had answered a serious religious question properly and professionally. What would make me really proud of myself was yet to come. That evening, just before supper, Lady Saria came back and had my answer confirmed by Father. She was duly impressed. From then on, I would be Lady Saria's trusted, easy-to-reach source for answers in Father's absence—until my family moved out of the neighborhood. For a while, I proudly thought to myself that I would perhaps make a genuine source of emulation one day. Father was not very encouraging when I mentioned the idea. "It takes more than just storing routine information to be a real man of God," he said.

NOW, THREE YEARS AFTEr Lady Saria's first acknowledgement of my scholarly skills, the answer books for the faithful were of renewed interest to me and my friends Habib and Hussen, all about 14 years old. One reason was Kasravi's writings, which we were secretly reading. They contained disparaging remarks about the venerable authors of these family guidebooks, making us eager to check the books again, first-hand. Another reason was that we were all on the verge of puberty, and certain passages in the guidebooks now sounded relevant. For one thing, we had noticeable facial hair now, which entailed discussions on the forthcoming, inevitable, beard-and-mustache problem: to shave or not to shave. Hussen and I were definitely going to be clean-shaven, when the time came. Just like my older brothers and almost all of our school teachers. Habib, too, wanted very much to be a face-shaver when he grew up, but wasn't sure if this would be permissible. Habib's elders emulated a source different from my family's, and thus had a different handbook for their guidance. Their source absolutely forbade "deep shaving," that is, shaving with a razor. This was verifiably the way of heathens, their handbook asserted, definitely to be avoided by the faithful at all cost.

Fortunately for me, and for my older brothers before me, the guidebook in my household permitted deep shaving, although my father himself preferred to sport a modest three-day growth. (I have wondered sometimes how he, who considered any adherence to current fashions but a clear and loud sign of shallowness, and a definite defect in personality, react to the extreme fashionability of his beard style among the cool young men-about-town, half a century after his death.) Hussen had no such worries, he said, after he confessed to us that his uncle, his guardian ever since his father's death, was quite liberal when it came to these matters, although he did "own a guidebook for appearances' sake." This was shocking news to me. Was his uncle also liberal on the subject of Kasravi and his teachings, I asked Hussen. Did he agree with Kasravi, for example, that visiting the sacred shrines, with the purpose of pleading with departed Imams and saints to cure an ailment, is a useless act? Did his uncle reject, as Kasravi did, our faith in the Twelfth Infallible Imam? And our belief that the Imam, born more than a thousand years ago, was still living but hidden from almost all mortal eyes? "I think not," Hussen said to my relief, "I remember my uncle getting very upset with a young friend who had praised Kasravi at a dinner party at our place." What did the friend say? I was curious to know. Hussen recalled the shocking statements by the young man: "He said it wasn't surprising that Kasravi was killed by superstitious illiterates, because he was two hundred years ahead of his stupid fellow countrymen. He said the Government was pleased with the killing; in fact the killers were pardoned by the Shah. The young man also compared Kasravi to other religious reformers in our ancient history, especially Mazdak, who was murdered, he said, by an alliance of the fanatic clergy and the ruling class." Wow! What kind of friends were entertained in Hussen's household! No family circle seemed to be immune any longer to unbelief and blasphemy.

The three of us went back to the guidebooks in our respective households, and looked for questions and answers concerning blasphemers. To be sure, some sins came with specific punishments authorized in these books, some of which my friends and I found curious. (A prime example of this—new to me, because it was certainly not in *my* family's answer book—we found among the edicts given by the source emulated by Habib's parents. It concerned this question: what to do if a shepherd has had sexual intercourse with a sheep, a member of his herd? The man had to be punished of course, we knew, but we didn't find this fact too interesting. But the sheep, said the answer book in Habib's household, was not fit to milk; nor was it fit to slaughter for food. It had to be killed and its body burned. This didn't sound too unreasonable to us. It was the answer to the natural question that followed, admittedly an ingenious answer, which really impressed us also as a practical one in the circumstances. Question: What if the herd was very large and the indecent sheep got away and was unrecognizable in the midst of all its innocent comrades? Answer: Divide the herd into two groups, as equal as possible. Toss a coin to exempt one of the two groups. Divide the other group into two halves again, toss a coin, and repeat the procedure, until two sheep are left. Toss a final coin and exempt one. Then kill and burn the remaining sheep.)

None of our three families' essential reference books said anything about punishments for blasphemers. We would learn years later that Kasravi's murder was sanctioned by several sources of emulation, but for now, all we found in our household books was how unclean certain blasphemers were. "*Najes*" was the technical word for the kind of unclean we are talking about, when applied to a person, an animal, or an object. The kind that necessitates a ritual washing and cleansing. The book of answers in my household listed several categories of najes, such as wine, dogs, and unbelievers. All of this I knew. But the text had another category, which had escaped my attention before: Even "a believer who curses, or expresses enmity towards, one of our twelve Infallible Imams is najes," the book said. Surely, Habib and I decided, Kasravi qualified. He had refuted the belief in the very existence of the Twelfth Imam. The Imam who was born in the year 869 A.D., was in and out of sight for a while, last disappeared in 941, and was now awaiting the Almighty's permission to make a final appearance before the end of time. Kasravi had also rejected the believers' faith in the superhuman powers of the twelve Imams altogether. He had denied that the Imams performed supernatural acts, and had even made fun of them. "Let us believe the miracle stories for a moment," Kasravi had written, "let us believe

that, as reported by the chroniclers, the Sixth Imam did talk
to a lizard and that the lizard did reply to him in fluent
and literate Arabic. But then it is the lizard who should get
credit for the miracle, not the Imam." The book of rebuttals
to Kasravi's claims, which I'd brought home to Father's
unexpected disapproval, said that this statement was both
unfunny and illogical, and the miracle was clearly not in the
talking but in causing the lizard to talk. "Let us see Kasravi
himself make a lizard talk if he can," the pious author wrote
mockingly, "now that he thinks of himself as one chosen by
God to lead us." Amizrahim the bookseller was in amused
agreement with Kasravi on the matter of miracles, but not
on everything. "The Prophet himself explicitly confessed
often," Amizrahim said to me and my friends, "that he was
an ordinary servant of God like us, and that he was not
capable of performing any miracles." Amizrahim was sure
that Kasravi was a true believer, though misguided about
certain issues. "These so-called scholars could have tried to
prove him wrong, if they disagreed with him," he said, "but
have him murdered?"

"Pure garbage!" said Hussen after he read the rebuttal
book. Habib and I thought it had some points to ponder, but
it had certainly failed to accomplish its intended mission for
us. We would look elsewhere for proper answers to Kasravi's
sinful thoughts, we decided. But we agreed on one thing with
Amizrahim: To erase blasphemy, there must be a better way
than murder, even if this had long been the preferred way to
silence blasphemers. We remembered what the dinner guest
had said to Hussen's uncle about the murder of Mazdak the
reformer, 1400 years ago: that it was an alliance between the

Royal Court and the Church which had led to it. Mazdak had also been accused, as Kasravi had, of false prophecy for God. He had also said things that were considered as blasphemous by the official church of the land at the time. So, we asked ourselves, was Kasravi the new Mazdak? Our interest in Mazdak, who had been mentioned but dismissively in our history lessons, had suddenly heightened. "There is an old book in my house," I said to my friends, "that has a detailed account of Mazdak's execution. And you know its famous author."

I was referring to the *Siasatnameh,* or "Book of Government." It has been compared to "The Prince" by Machiavelli. Half a millennium before Machiavelli, it was written by one of the best-known political administrators in Iranian history, Nizam al-Mulk, the powerful grand vizier to two kings for a total of thirty years. It is a guidebook for Kings. On how to rule and how to behave like a king; whom to favor, whom to ignore, whom to exile, and whom to kill. Also, incidentally, on whom to party with, how, when, and how often. (To my extreme shock—since the author is such a staunch adherent to the Faith—the book even contains a chapter on how to serve wine at the court parties. The only explanation I, as a kid, could come up with was, well, a king is an exception to every rule: he can do as he pleases, and that is why he is called king.) The book teaches by example. One example that had made a great impression on me when I first read it, was the story of justice dispensed on heretics by the legendary Sassanid emperor, Anushirvan the Just. Now that my interest was rekindled, I read it again. After four years—a very long stretch when you are a kid.

Anushirvan was still the Crown prince when his father, the reigning emperor of Iran, came under the influence of Mazdak, who was by the Siasatnameh's account, the ungodly proponent of sharing wealth and women by all men. Mazdak led a rebellion against the extra-ordinary power of orthodox Zoroastrian priests in the sixth century—he has been described as a proto-communist by some modern historians. Anushirvan and his court priests, the book tells us, knew what a potential danger Mazdak and his 12,000 followers posed for the empire. Together they staged some theological debates between Mazdak and themselves, which the priests won, of course. But this proved less than satisfactory as Mazdak's followers seemed to be fast increasing in numbers. So they decided to play a trick on the Mazdakists, a means well justified by their pious aims: They announced that the emperor had decided to accept the new faith as the official state religion; and that, to celebrate this historic occasion, there would be a sumptuous open-air party on the Court grounds, where Mazdak would be His Majesty's guest of honor. The date for the auspicious occasion was announced. All members of the new movement were invited to attend from the four corners of the vast empire. They were now officially proclaimed to be the chosen people among the emperor's subjects, "those lucky enough to see the light ahead of their fellow countrymen."

Every one of them, says the Book of Government, came on the appointed day. Mazdzk himself was placed on a luxurious pedestal, steps above every court priest. The guests were wined and dined lavishly. Then they were promised prizes to remember the day by: new uniforms, bejeweled swords, and more. In order to be properly outfitted and to receive personalized rewards, they were then escorted away from the party grounds in groups of twenty or thirty. As soon as each group entered a gated inner courtyard, however, each happy guest was grabbed by a skilled imperial guard and buried alive, vertically and upside down, from head to knee, in one of the holes neatly dug and readied the day before. (Here I remembered with embarrassment how differently I had reacted to the gruesome account, when I first read it. I remembered the glee with which I had rooted for those agents of righteousness: "Send them to Hell fast, those infidels!"—Not unlike a kid caught in the excitement of winning a video game by machine-gunning all the villains on the screen.) When the time came for Mazdak himself to leave the party and go through the fatal gate, he was first treated to the surprise of his life: the green grounds he now entered had grown 12,000 pairs of legs, some still dangling in the air. He was then led to his own hole, in the center of a wide and high platform. And he was buried, alive just like his followers, but the right side up in his case. So, the faithful royal guests had an opportunity to participate in the sacred cleansing of the empire by throwing stones to smash Mazdak's head and dismember his upper body. Thus it was, the book says, that Anushirvan succeeded in putting an end to this poisonous movement, after which he immediately dethroned and imprisoned his father for his recent misguided sympathies, and started to rule the empire himself, with a mighty hand. And always justly.

HABIB AND HUSSEN BORROWED THE BOOK of Government from me and read its Mazdak story for the first time. Hussen hadn't heard about it at all. But Habib remembered hearing it as a child. It was retold, he said, by a clergyman, during a sermon in connection with false prophets and their just punishments. Habib also remembered his happy reaction to the story—very similar to mine—upon hearing that the infidels got what they deserved. Hussen was puzzled by the embarrassed remembrances Habib and I were exchanging. And by our palpable fears. "Are we losing our faith?" Habib asked me, echoing my own sentiments, "Our feelings are so different from just a few years ago about killing unbelievers. What is next? Are we being slowly led off the right path? Are we going to end up, God forbid, as Hell-bound apostates?" The more we thought, the more anxious we became: Should we perhaps not indulge so much in reading, our greatest passion? Could Lady Saria the Pious possibly be right in warning everybody who listened to her about the evils of excessive reading? Didn't she quote her reliable scholarly sources on the real reason why Ali, the local grocer's son, was now in a mental hospital? That all this suffering could have been avoided if only Ali had listened to repeated warnings by wiser men? If only he had stopped reading those ungodly verses written by Omar Khayyam?

Habib and I did not dare discuss our fears with our elders. So, we decided to consult Amizrahim, the bookseller. Naturally. The situation was too desperate for Habib to worry about the risk of being seen by his father's associates in the bazaar. When we arrived at the bookstore, Amizrahim and his sons were having their afternoon tea break. He asked his younger son to pour us some tea. He was his usual kind, fatherly, trustworthy, and serene self. He wasn't surprised at all when he heard about the cause of our distress. He listened and smiled. He understood.

"I promise you," Amizrahim said, consoling us and easing our fear of reading. "If you ever lose your faith, it won't be because you are opposed to killing the people who express doubts. Or because you read books by those who disagree with you. Besides, would I want to lose two of my best customers?"

Dreaming of Free Elections

"His Majesty has decided to allow free elections in our city," said my new colleague Ali. He was obviously very excited, and happy to share the good news with us, a group of professors having tea at the faculty cafeteria. Most of us were only amused. We had already heard, and readily dismissed, the rumors about an imminent royal experiment with free parliamentary elections. We were all members of the Faculty of Arts and Science at Pahlavi University—so named, of course, after His Imperial Majesty, the Shah of Iran. The city was Shiraz, and the year was 1971.

Ali had recently returned from the United States with his brand-new doctorate in hand, and his young American bride in tow, to join the faculty. But everybody else at the tea had been in Shiraz for a few years at least. Most of the faculty members were, unlike Ali, completely disillusioned with politics since the early 50s' upheavals. My friends and I were resigned to our roles as teachers of science and technology to the next generation. Politically radical students considered our attitude cowardly. And they forgave only those of us who were demonstrably apolitical. That is, those of us who avoided all higher administrative positions, quietly boycotted all "elections," and stayed away from the political "parties." There were only two legal parties in the country; both approved personally by His Imperial Majesty and thus allowed to exist above ground. People in such circles as ours mockingly referred to them, when no party members were within earshot, as "the Yes Party" and "the Of-course Party".

"We *are* cowards," said my good friend Hamed, "and we know it." He reminded us that we'd done nothing and said nothing in public, for example, when a certain young, politically active member of the faculty was imprisoned without trial and later exiled to a college in a faraway city. We had justified ourselves by the conviction that doing anything or saying anything, would be counter-productive under the circumstances. What would our students gain, what would anybody gain, my friends argued, if we spoke out and went to prison ourselves? Did we want to make room in the University for illiterate sycophants, those individuals more acceptable and more useful to the center of power? Obviously not, it had been decided almost unanimously. Even the jailed professor himself seemed to concur, according to Hamed. "When I accidentally met him at my dentist's office a few weeks ago," Hamed told us, "he had just been released from prison and was to be banished from Shiraz. He looked pale and frightened. I couldn't help wondering if his teeth were, as rumored, broken under torture; and if, after the extraction of requisite confessions from him in prison, his inquisitors had arranged for a grant toward the required dental reconstruction. I hoped to God, of course, that the rumors were false. I did want to ask him, but he kept our conversation to an absolute minimum. 'It wouldn't be good for either of us' he whispered, 'if we were seen together or communicated at all, in case our paths happened to cross again in the near future.' And he left the clinic as fast as he could."

We'd assumed that Ali was one of us. So we were surprised that there was no note of irony in his statement about the coming free elections. Then he really shocked us by announcing his own candidacy for membership of the National Parliament from Shiraz. He clearly believed that the next round of elections would be free, exclusively in Shiraz of course, as an experiment. "His Majesty couldn't have chosen a more suitable site for the trial," he said. "With its obviously manageable size and relatively well-educated, moderate, easy-going population, Shiraz has a huge advantage over bigger cities with unpredictable inhabitants that include a fair number of religious fanatics."

An older and wiser colleague tried to advise Ali against his planned adventure. "You must be aware," he said to Ali, "that this would require, before you are even allowed to run, a thorough investigation by the SAVAK." (This was the well-known Persian acronym for the powerful Organization of Intelligence and National Security.) He was sure that they would invade the privacy of every member of Ali's extended family in search of what they considered indications of possibly treasonous activities. But Ali was resolute about running. He had done nothing wrong, he stated confidently, and he was open to any investigation by the authorities into his spotless past. And he was determined to serve the people of Shiraz, now that free elections were being promised at last, at least in his city.

Ali had to leave the tea session early, but the rest of us couldn't stop thinking about his announcement. "He is bound to come to his senses soon," predicted one colleague. "Just give him a little time." Most of us nodded in agreement, and then tried to make light of the situation—this was our recently acquired habit, our automatic reaction to official propaganda. "Let us assume for the moment," said Hamed, "that the rumors about this local experiment with free elections, laughable though they sound, were true. If you were in His Majesty's shoes, looking for a good-sized city for a trial run, you must agree with Ali that Shiraz would be an excellent choice." Everyone seemed to be willing to step into His Majesty's shoes for the purpose of this discussion. "Tehran is clearly out of the question," offered a Tehrani colleague. "How can you trust a population that came so close to electing an all-communist list of candidates for the Parliament a mere twenty years ago, before His Majesty decided that enough was enough and that we weren't yet ready for such luxuries as free elections?" Colleagues from Isfahan and Mashad also thought their big cities unsuitable for the forthcoming experiment on account of their very traditional and religious populations. I was sure, as well, about my own home city. "I would certainly not choose Tabriz over Shiraz," I said "because we Azeris are an easily excitable tribe, as you are all so fond of reminding us at every opportunity you get to tell a 'Turkish' joke. His Majesty would have to worry about us getting into heated arguments in the streets of Tabriz, if exposed to a free-election experiment." Then I told them of my own recent experience in Shiraz, this city of romantic poets and peace-loving inhabitants, where I had lived for four years without witnessing a single street quarrel among its citizens.

Open squabbles, especially after a traffic accident, were not uncommon in the narrow streets of Tabriz, where I spent the first eighteen years of my life. When I was growing up, there weren't many motor vehicles in the city. But horse-driven carts and donkeys ran into each other more than occasionally, causing damage to a leg or a wheel. This would invariably result in loud and heated arguments, attracting curious spectators. A random spectator, chosen only on the basis of ripe age and respectable looks, would sometimes be drafted to act as an impromptu mediator and judge. I must have missed these street scenes during my years away from Tabriz: it was almost a nostalgic experience when I finally spotted a street altercation in Shiraz, between the drivers of a car and a truck. I have to see this closely, I said to myself; I have to hear their local fighting words in their special, relaxed dialect of Persian; Persian as spoken by Shirazis, whom I'd come to regard as habitually laid-back and fun-loving citizens who avoided trouble at any cost. Alas, I was disappointed once I was close enough to hear the angry words: they were uttered by both parties, not in Persian at all, but in very fluent and familiar Azeri Turkish that could only come from the native speakers in my own city or its immediate environs. For a fleeting moment, I considered offering my services as a mediator who spoke their language, but I wasn't really old enough, and didn't have a respectable-looking beard.

"THIS IS NO LAUGHING MATTER," said a colleague after hearing my story. "Ali is bound to get hurt, if not before the elections, then definitely after—assuming that he is permitted to run at all—and especially if he is allowed to win. He'll think of course that his election was fair and proper. And he'll behave accordingly, which will certainly be unforgivable by the Shah's men. Don't you remember the former leader of the Of-Course Party, who started to believe that he was actually leading a true opposition group?" We did remember: This was a distinguished former parliamentarian who was recently forced to leave politics altogether, because he had forgotten to ask for the Shah's personal permission before openly suggesting minor changes to the land-reform program spearheaded by His Majesty himself.

We agreed that we should all try to dissuade Ali and make him think again of his job as an educator, and of his family, before acting on his fantasy. Fortunately, the elections were still a few months away. We ordered more tea and biscuits; nobody was ready to leave yet. "We as a nation deserve no better, anyway," opined Karim, one of our more cynical friends. "How large a fraction of our population— yes, even in large and supposedly enlightened cities like Shiraz—do you think so much as knows the meaning of free elections?" He went on to prove his point: "Remember all those street demonstrations we took part in when we were young? All those huge banners we carried on our shoulders? All those lofty, radical messages on the banners? Well, I am a little older than you guys and I remember a few more of those demonstrations, and I remember them well. You no doubt recall the popular slogans that started with 'Long Live' and 'Death to.' Some of the banners my friends and I carried said 'Death to Exploitation!' or 'Death to Reaction!' and some mentioned specific people by name. One of those people, you surely remember, was Seyyed Zia. That well known, controversial, old-fashioned, aged politician, who'd played such a huge role in the coup of 1921, but was exiled almost right away by the nation's new boss who would soon be king. As you know, Seyyed Zia made a comeback in the early Forties, after the old King, the one who had outsmarted him, was himself sent to exile once the Allies occupied the country in 1941. And then he founded an ultraconservative party and became a symbol of evil to us young revolutionaries. Well, the banner I was carrying during a hot-summer-day demonstration said 'Death to Seyyed Zia!' A spectator, a very old man who could barely read, recognized Seyyed Zia's name, as one to be hated. He had no problem with that slogan. But 'exploitation' and 'reaction' were unfamiliar words to him. 'Who is this Reaction?' he asked innocently, addressing one of my comrades who happened to be carrying a large banner that said 'Death to Reaction.' The banner holder started to explain what it meant as patiently as he could. But he soon had to give up in frustration. 'It is just Seyyed Zia's brother,' he said finally, to the apparent satisfaction of the inquirer."

"Exactly," agreed Samad Agha, another colleague, even older and more cynical than Karim, "I myself had a chance to sell my vote for a good lunch in the mid-forties, when His Majesty, quite young at the time, was apparently still content to reign as a constitutional monarch, and when elections were ostensibly free. One of the rich landowners in my town was running for Parliament. His servants simply went around the bazaar and gave generous lunch coupons to those willing to lend them their National ID cards for a couple of hours. The lender didn't even have to go to the polling station. The servants simply used the card to vote—

the ID cards didn't have pictures in those days—and had it stamped as required by law, and returned it to the lender before the lunch was served. So, you see, since eighty-five percent of our population is still practically illiterate, what sense do free elections make anyway? Shouldn't we just relax and concentrate on educating the nation's youth? And be satisfied, for the time being, with the Parliament members selected on our behalf by His Majesty and his trusted advisors?"

"Not too many free lunches are given these days," said Karim, "now that the parliament members have no real power at all; they are told which bills to vote for and which to vote against. I suppose they just enjoy the empty title and the not-so-empty purse that go with the job. Is our young colleague Ali hoping to be an exception? Can he be? Let us be realists, for God's sake."

Samad Agha's tone got more serious. "Let us not kid ourselves," he admonished us young and inexperienced citizens, "Karim is quite right. We don't deserve any better government than we've got." Samad Agha knew how much we liked and respected him, and he didn't care if not everybody agreed with his views on recent Iranian history. He just wished, he said, that we had learned from the lessons of our many past revolutions and coups. "Let us assume," he further elaborated, "that, all of a sudden, free elections became a reality right now. Shall we? Just for argument's sake? Okay, What kind of politicians do you think will be elected as a result? What kind of government do you hope to end up with? I'll tell you what kind: You are only dreaming like children if you think we'll get a social democracy! The only realistic outcome will be a full-blown theocracy! The obvious reason is that for now the clergy has the widest power base among our illiterate masses. Amend your dreams friends! This is how it'll end: the Parliament will be filled with clerics! And before you know it, you'll have a government much more authoritarian than the current one."

"How so?" a young colleague asked. "How can the conditions possibly get more politically repressive than they are now?" Samad Agha gave him one of his familiar older-and-wiser-than-you smiles. "Yes, you are right, of course," he said, "we have no political freedom. But think of all the little things you are free to do now, all those everyday things. I'll give you just one example: You and I, together with our better halves, enjoyed our dinner and drinks at this nice new restaurant on Zand Avenue last weekend. Right then and there, we innocently committed three sinful acts, each severely punishable under the hypothetical theocracy I am warning you against." Everybody was all ears as Samad Agha went on in a more serious, almost lecturing mode. "Number one: consumption of alcohol. Two: free mixing of genders unprotected by hijab. And three: doing all this during the fasting month of Ramazan! Imagine! I am old enough to remember that our village mullah once ordered a man killed just for not observing his fasting duties in Ramazan." (A decade later, having witnessed the 1979 Revolution and the restrictions the new regime would impose on his personal life, a very old and infirm Samad Agha would whisper a soft reminder to his trusted friends among the younger gener-ation, at any chance he got, that he had told them so.)

OUR THOUGHTS TURNED BACK to our colleague Ali and the unavoidable predicament he was stepping into. Sighs were emitted in concern for Ali's future. Everybody was in agreement that our incumbent parliamentarians had no real power to speak of; except, perhaps, when it came to procuring Government jobs or contracts for their friends and relatives. They'd heard many second-hand stories, not all entirely reliable, they said. But I had a first-hand account of a recent adventure of mine, which I now related to them: my trip to Poland to attend a mathematics conference.

This was in the previous summer. By the time I made up my mind to go to the conference, I had only a month to make arrangements. And, I knew, getting Government permission to travel to an Iron-Curtain country was not a routine matter. I decided to enlist the help of a Member of Parliament from Shiraz whom I knew—and who, incidentally, had also been a professor at Pahalavi University in Shiraz. I visited him in his office in the capital, Tehran. He was delighted to see his old colleague, he said, and ordered the customary tea and biscuits for me. He looked very busy, carrying simultaneous conversations with several constituents present in his spacious office, all at different stages of consuming their teas and biscuits. As soon as I spoke the words "exit" and "visa," he waited for no further explanation from this constituent. He was eager to help. "Why didn't you come to me earlier?" he asked me in friendly admonishment, "I have a *carte blanch* with the Director of the Central Passport Bureau." He called one of his assistants and ordered him to take me directly to the Passport Bureau downtown. The assistant helpfully drove me there, mentioned the parliamentarian's name, and instantly got me an audience with the director himself. The director turned out to be an army general, around retirement age, impressively dressed in uniform and wearing a monocle. He was sitting regally on a high chair behind an inordinately huge desk. He did not move from his chair, but graciously greeted me with a smile and ordered a cup of tea for me. What could he do for me and his friend the parliamentarian, he asked. He sounded sincere and willing to please. But once I mentioned Poland, he was uncomfortable. "As you must know," he said with a darkened but sympathetic expression, "this cannot be done so fast. This is a national security matter. It is really out of our hands." He showed his empty hands and clapped very gently, only his fingertips touching. Then he lowered his voice and spoke of the all-powerful security folk at the SAVAK, who had the final say on every trip to the other side of the Curtain. "And it would take many weeks if not months," he added. "So, I would cancel the trip if I were you," he advised me. When we parted, the general was obviously embarrassed at his impotence to act on the recommendation of his friend. And I was embarrassed for both of them, the Parliament Member from Shiraz, and the Director of the Central Passport Bureau.

Since I had already—quite foolishly, I must admit— bought my air ticket for the Warsaw trip and I really wanted to go, I consulted a friend who claimed to know about the workings of His Imperial Majesty's Secret Service. "Go to the Dean of Students at the University," he said, reminding me that the dean and I knew each other well from our university days. "He is certain to have the right connections and I am sure he can solve your problem. Because of the political sensitivity of his position in dealing with dissident students, he's got to be assumed trustworthy by the SAVAK." Excellent advice, I thought, and I took it. As soon as I met the dean that very morning, and mentioned my problem, he left a telephone message for the Security Chief himself, the most feared man in the SAVAK, no less. A reply came in less than fifteen minutes from the chief's secretary, directing me back to the Passport Bureau, where I was to bypass the director's fancy office and pick up my exit visa from the discreet little SAVAK branch office; directly, without fuss. So I was able to go to my conference behind the Iron Curtain, after all.

"You must tell it to Ali!" one colleague urged me when he heard my story. And I did, first chance I had, the next day. "But times have changed since last summer," Ali said with obvious conviction, "and now the parliamentarians will get the respect they deserve, once they are freely elected by the people."

THANKS TO THE POLITICALLY NEUTRAL state of mathematics and natural sciences, most of us at Pahlavi University continued to keep our relatively undisturbed heads in the sand. Not a single faculty member had yet been pressured to join either political party. Those very few from our ranks who were known as either Yessers or Of-coursers, had chosen their paths of their own accord. There seemed to be an unwritten pact between the bulk of us academics and the Establishment: we stayed away from politics, and they left us alone. Being left alone was a privilege indeed. And not many government employees were entitled to it: High school teachers, for example, seemed to be under great pressure to educate their students on the principles of His Majesty's White Revolution. We the professors, except for those few who travelled in higher circles, took great advantage of this unwritten non-aggression pact between us and the Establishment.

But things began to change. All around us, there appeared clear indications that the unwritten pact we'd been so resolutely clinging to wouldn't last. An advocate of the Royal White Revolution with a new administrative appointment at the University, arrived on the scene. Either a Yesser or an Of-courser, I don't remember which. He kept asserting at every academic gathering that "certain educators among us" need to clarify their positions, once and for all. "You can't keep a full jar tilted and not spill the juice," he warned the faculty members. He was employing a well-worn Persian proverb to chide us. "Straighten the jar or spill the juice. Make up your mind, make a choice!" It was his patriotic duty, he insisted, to make this clear to "all our nation's educators." He didn't name names. But we, the cautious holders of half-tilted juice jars, were naturally disturbed by his pronouncements. His wasn't the only loud voice. In fact, the general population of the country was now being fed a constant diet of praise for the great leader, the *Shahanshah*, King of Kings, Light of the Aryans, through the state-controlled media. Even young kids were included in the ceaseless indoctrination through the national radio and television. I once asked the four-year old son of a relative if he knew what this word "Shah" meant, this word that was constantly in the air. "It means God," he said without hesitation. "If the Shah were here now," I said, "he would give you a big medal." "But if God were here," added his father, "He would give you a big kick in the butt."

When it finally happened at our university, we were not too surprised: A circular came from the Dean of the Faculty of Arts and Science one afternoon. It was addressed to every faculty member. It informed us that on the coming Wednesday, at 10 a.m., a prayer session would be held for His Majesty's continued health. The announced location was the Shah-Cheragh mosque—the most important Shrine in Southern Iran, which housed the sacred mausoleum of the Eighth Infallible Imam's two brothers. "It is fitting," the official, typewritten message said, "that you attend the ceremonies in the name of our university community."

"It is fitting that you do what we suggest you do." How I always hated this expression in official messages—even far back, when they came from the principal's office while I was in high school! It was understood to imply more than just "strongly recommended." It pretty much meant "you better do it." My friend Hamed and I had to agree now that this missive from the dean smacked of a unilateral termination of our unwritten pact with the Establishment. We had no intension of participating in this forced show of affection, in "this circus," as Hamed put it. But, as cowards, we looked for a safe way out. And we thought we'd found one: The prayer session in the shrine was scheduled not for a weekend—as it had been the usual practice so far on occasions of this sort— but for a regular week day, when we had scheduled classes to teach. Good cover. Except that the dean, or whoever ordered the dean around, had foreseen this potential excuse on our part, as we discovered upon reading the form letter more thoroughly: the second paragraph explicitly stated that all Wednesday morning classes would be cancelled for our convenience.

So Hamed and I stayed at my home together during that morning. While the praying went on in the shrine, we busied ourselves with marking our students' homework papers. It was an anxious, harrowing morning. And, as it turned out, it would play a last-straw role in putting an end to my career at Pahlavi University. Hamed and I couldn't concentrate on our marking task; we worried about the consequences of our disobedience. We kept the radio on. It was of course broadcasting the group prayers live, for the benefit of the general citizenry. We listened and tried to gauge the size of the crowd at the shrine by the sound of the collective amens. We hoped for high attendance, which would make our own absence inconspicuous. We confessed to each other that the situation wasn't helping our sense of self-esteem at all. We walked to school in the afternoon and did our best to act as if nothing had changed. We were relieved that nobody asked questions about the morning. But nobody seemed quite at ease either. I remember my own state of mind vividly. It was not an enviable state of mind: that afternoon I wished that I were either sufficiently in favor of His Majesty's autocratic rule to have attended the prayer ceremonies, or sufficiently against it to have been in prison.

For several days afterwards, Hamed and I privately discussed the morality of neutrality. But more urgent for us now was not the morality, but the tenability, of neutrality while employed as educators. What would we do the next time they decided that it was "fitting" for us to show our unconditional and heartfelt agreement with His Majesty's whims? Would we be permitted again, I asked Hamed, to hide in our homes while wishing that a large enough number of our colleagues had *not* resorted to the same trick? Hamed thought I was taking this whole situation a little too seriously, being a little "too logical, too mathematical about it," as he put it. Mathematical or not, the situation became the a topic of serious family deliberations for the next few weeks, and a decision was soon made. Then I wrote to Peter, my friend and colleague in Toronto, whom I had visited several times to work on our joint research projects. I told him that my family and I were planning to come back to Canada—this time to stay.

I SAT IN A CAFÉ WITH ALI after school one late afternoon at the end of that Spring term, my last year of teaching at Pahlavi University. The most recent parliamentary elections had come and gone. It had been a busy school term, and there hadn't been an opportunity for me to talk with Ali in person. But I'd been assured by common friends that he had decided not to run after all. When Ali learned about my imminent departure for Canada, he told me that he, too, was leaving the University and the country. I was surprised. "But what happened to your political ambitions, your candidacy?" I had to ask. "Well, it is a long story," he whispered, "but I'll give you a short version." He ordered another beer, as if to collect his courage for revealing a secret. "I went through all the prerequisites, you know, and was ready to stand for election," he said, watching the neighboring tables to make sure nobody was eavesdropping, "but I had to invent a family excuse to withdraw my candidacy at the very last minute."

"But Why?" I asked. "Why? Weren't you the optimist among us?" I had obviously touched a sore spot. "Hush, hush!" he whispered, "I had gone through all the preliminaries, and was ready to go, when the SAVAK guys respectfully put this neatly typewritten letter before me and asked me to sign it. It was just a minor formality, they said, and they wouldn't worry about it at all if they were me. They assured me that every candidate had to sign a similar form." Ali looked very angry now, and asked me to guess what it was. It was a declaration of absolute allegiance to His Majesty, I guessed. A natural, but not entirely correct, guess. "No," he said. "It was my formal letter of resignation from the Parliament." I was puzzled, and Ali could see it. "It was undated," he explained. "The date would be filled in, they told me, 'only if and when it proved necessary, God forbid.'"